שׂפתי תפתח

Siddur Mastery & Meaning

David's Harp

David was a very busy king. He had almost no time for himself. During the day he took care of the people's needs. During every free moment he tried to squeeze in time to study Torah. David knew that the Torah would give him the wisdom he needed to rule well. Late at night he crawled into bed. Every night he hung his harp over his bed. In the middle of the night the north wind would begin to blow. The wind would move the strings. Slowly a melody would emerge. When that happened, David would wake up and sing with his harp. He would add words and create his psalms. These were David's prayers. He learned how to praise God by listening to his harp. (*Brakhot 3b*)

Questions

1. What lesson about prayer can you learn from this story?
2. When have you had a moment that is like this story?
3. How can knowing this story help you learn how to pray?

We wish to thank
Judy Aronson, Debi Rowe,
Ronit-Ben Shoshan, Micha'el Akiba
and Joshua Barkin
who worked with us and offered
invaluable insights on this project

by Joel Lurie Grishaver & Jane Golub

Artwork by Lane Yerkes, Christine Tripp, Mark Robert Halper & David Bleicher

Design by Alan Rowe

ISBN #1-891662-13-9

Torah Aura Productions • 4423 Fruitland Avenue, Los Angeles, CA 90058

(800) BE-Torah • (800) 238-6724 • (323) 585-7312 • fax (323) 585-0327

E-MAIL <misrad@torahaura.com> • Visit the Torah aura website at www.torahaura.com

MANUFACTURED IN CANADA

אֲדֹנָי שְׂפָתַי תִּפְתָּח

These words are a warm-up. They come from a poem written by King David (*Psalms* 51.17). It came from a moment when King David was having a lot of trouble knowing how to pray. Just as David spoke them to God as a way of beginning his prayer, we do the same.

Levi Yitzhak of Berdichev explained that in the days when the עֲמִידָה was first created, these words were not part of it. He taught, In those days, people knew how to point their hearts and feel close to God. In our day, אֲדֹנָי שְׂפָתַי תִּפְתָּח has been added as a prayer to get us ready to pray.

When God created Adam and Eve, God breathed into them the spirit of speech (*Targum*, Gen. 2.7). Words are the things that make people different from animals. Words are our special gift.

This prayer takes us back to the first people and asks God to help us use our words.

The Rabbis teach that two things make it hard for us to sincerely pray the עֲמִידָה:

We don't feel that we are good enough to deserve God's help. We are afraid thaT things we have done wrong will bother God too much. We are afraid that God won't help us.

We are afraid to admit that we need help. To pray the עֲמִידָה we have to admit that we have problems we cannot fix on our own.

The Talmud teaches us that God gave us the power to speak so that we could say we are sorry and so that we could ask for what we need. אֲדֹנָי שְׂפָתַי תִּפְתָּח helps us remember this.

In this unit you will learn:

• the introduction to the עֲמִידָה

• נֶגֶד פָּתַח הַלֵּל

• A King David Story

3

Can you see the three letters פתח in these words?

תְּפַתַּח   פּוֹתֵחַ   פִּתְחוּ

Hebrew builds words out of three-letter roots.

You will open = תְּפַתַּח

open = פּוֹתֵחַ

Open! = פִּתְחוּ

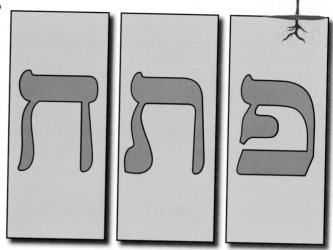

Practice these phrases and circle all the words that contain the root פתח.

1. פִּתְחוּ לִי שַׁעֲרֵי צֶדֶק   (פּוֹתֵחַ) אֶת יָדֶךָ וּמַשְׂבִּיעַ לְכָל חַי רָצוֹן

2. אֲדֹנָי שְׂפָתַי (תִּפְתָּח) אֲנִי-עַבְדְּךָ בֶּן-אֲמָתֶךָ (פִּתַּחְתָּ) לְמוֹסֵרִי

Can you see the three letters נגד in these words?

הַגָּדָה   מַגִּיד   יַגִּיד

Hebrew builds words out of three-letter roots.
Notice that with this root, the נ falls out.

will tell = יַגִּיד

the telling = מַגִּיד

Haggadah = הַגָּדָה

Practice these words and circle all the words that contain the root נגד.

3. שְׂפָתַי (לְהַגִּיד) (אֲדֹנָי) (הַגָּדָה) אֲמוֹתֵינוּ (הַגֵּד) (יַגִּיד)

4. תְּפַתַּח וּפִי (הַגִּיד) תְּהִלָּתֶךָ (מַגִּיד) חֲסָדִים

4

Can you see the three letters הלל in these words?

הַלֵּל   תְּהִלָּה   הַלְלוּיָהּ

Sometimes one of the ל letters falls out.

prayers of praise (psalms) = הַלֵּל

praises = תְּהִלָּה

Praise the Eternal! = הַלְלוּיָהּ

Practice these phrases and circle all the words that contain the root הלל.

1. הַלְלוּ עַבְדֵי יי   הַלְלוּ אֶת־שֵׁם יי   כֹּל הַנְּשָׁמָה תְּהַלֵּל יָהּ הַלְלוּיָהּ

2. הַלְלוּהוּ בְּנֵבֶל וְכִנּוֹר   הַלְלוּהוּ בְּתֵקַע שׁוֹפָר

3. בְּמִצְוֹתָיו וְצִוָּנוּ לִקְרֹא אֶת־הַהַלֵּל   מֶלֶךְ מְהֻלָּל בַּתִּשְׁבָּחוֹת

Words

God = אֲדֹנָי

Word Parts

and = וְ

your = ךָ

הַלֵּל

נָגִיד

פֶּה

פָּתַח

שְׂפָתַיִם

אֲדֹנָי שְׂפָתַי תִּפְתָּח וּפִי יַגִּיד תְּהִלָּתֶךָ

Your teacher will help you with your translation.

עֲצֹר!

My best guess at the meaning of this prayer is:

god open your llips to his mouth

5

Practice this line we are studying.

1. אֲדֹנָי שְׂפָתַי תִּפְתָּח וּפִי יַגִּיד תְּהִלָּתֶךָ

Here are some phrases from the עֲמִידָה to practice.

h

2. בָּרוּךְ אַתָּה יי אֱלֹהֵינוּ וֵאלֹהֵי אֲבוֹתֵינוּ וְאִמּוֹתֵינוּ

Alex

3. אַתָּה גִּבּוֹר לְעוֹלָם אֲדֹנָי מְחַיֶּה מֵתִים אַתָּה רַב לְהוֹשִׁיעַ

4. נְקַדֵּשׁ אֶת שִׁמְךָ בָּעוֹלָם כְּשֵׁם שֶׁמַּקְדִּישִׁים אוֹתוֹ בִּשְׁמֵי מָרוֹם

5. קָדוֹשׁ קָדוֹשׁ קָדוֹשׁ יי צְבָאוֹת מְלֹא כָל־הָאָרֶץ כְּבוֹדוֹ

6. וְטוֹב בְּעֵינֶיךָ לְבָרֵךְ אֶת עַמְּךָ יִשְׂרָאֵל בְּכָל עֵת וּבְכָל שָׁעָה בִּשְׁלוֹמֶךָ

7. שִׂים שָׁלוֹם טוֹבָה וּבְרָכָה חֵן וָחֶסֶד וְרַחֲמִים עָלֵינוּ

8. וְשָׁמְרוּ בְנֵי יִשְׂרָאֵל אֶת־הַשַּׁבָּת לַעֲשׂוֹת אֶת־הַשַּׁבָּת

9. הָאֵל הַגָּדוֹל הַגִּבּוֹר וְהַנּוֹרָא אֵל עֶלְיוֹן

10. שָׁלוֹם רָב עַל יִשְׂרָאֵל עַמְּךָ תָּשִׂים לְעוֹלָם

You support the falling, heal the ailling, free the letters

11. סוֹמֵךְ נוֹפְלִים וְרוֹפֵא חוֹלִים וּמַתִּיר אֲסוּרִים

12. יִמְלֹךְ יי לְעוֹלָם אֱלֹהַיִךְ צִיּוֹן לְדֹר וָדֹר הַלְלוּיָהּ

13. עֹשֶׂה שָׁלוֹם בִּמְרוֹמָיו הוּא יַעֲשֶׂה שָׁלוֹם עָלֵינוּ

King David
Messed Up
Big Time

It was the worst moment in King David's life (so far). It started one day when he went out on the roof of the palace and saw a really beautiful woman sunbathing. Immediately he fell in love with her. It didn't matter that she was married to someone else. David had to be with her even though it was wrong. He could not get her out of his head. This was a moment when   I want it   was stronger than   I know this is wrong.   David chose the wrong thing.

The woman's name was Batsheva, and her husband was one of David's soldiers. Even though she was married, David started spending time with her. Soon he had to have her for his own. David wrote to one of his generals. He had Batsheva's husband put in the lead in every battle in the place with the most danger. When he was killed, David took Batsheva as a wife.

Nathan was a prophet in David's court. One day he came to David with a story about a rich man with many sheep who stole a poor man's only sheep. David listened and felt bad. He said,   The rich man deserves to die.   Nathan pointed to David and said,   You are that man.   Then he said,   God is now very angry with you.

David suddenly realized how wrong he had been. He was really sorry. There was no way that he could bring Batsheva's husband back and make things right. He didn't know how to fix things. He also was afraid that God would never forgive him. There was now a huge space between him and God a big black hole. It was then that he sat down and wrote a poem, a prayer to God.

David began:

אֲדֹנָי שְׂפָתַי תִּפְתָּח וּפִי יַגִּיד תְּהִלָּתֶךָ.

He said, "God, I don't know how to begin. Words will not come. I want to talk to You, but I don't know what to say. I don't feel worthy." His prayer began, "Eternal, if You will open my lips and help me begin—then my tongue will find a way to pray to You." We all have times when we feel like David (*Midrash Tehillim 51; Bet Yosef on Tur 111-112*).

Questions

1. Why was it hard for David to pray to God when it was something he used to do every day?
2. Why did David write a prayer that asked for God's help in praying?
3. How does knowing this story help you to know how to get ready to pray the עֲמִידָה?

Reviewing שְׂפָתַי תִּפְתָּח

Some things to know about שְׂפָתַי תִּפְתָּח

- This sentence from the Psalms is used as a way to "warm up" and get in the right frame of mind and heart to pray the עֲמִידָה.
- This verse reminds us of a story about King David, who wrote it when he was really desperate.

Language Learning

Roots: הלל   נגד   פתח

Words:

 תְּהִלָּה   נַגִּיד   פֶּה   פָּתַח   שְׂפָתַיִם

עֲצֹר!

8

עֲמִידָה

The בְּרָכוֹת of the עֲמִידָה are where Jews do most of their deepest prayer work. The עֲמִידָה is a string of בְּרָכוֹת that are linked together to form the heart of the morning, afternoon, evening, and extra (מוּסָף) services. During the week the עֲמִידָה is made up of nineteen בְּרָכוֹת. On Shabbat there are seven.

Different communities pray the עֲמִידָה in different ways. Originally everyone stood, faced toward Jerusalem, took three steps forward, put their feet together, and said all the prayers in the עֲמִידָה silently without interruption. In the שַׁחֲרִית (morning), מִנְחָה (afternoon), and מוּסָף (extra) services the prayer leader then repeated the עֲמִידָה out loud. This did not happen in the evening. That is still the "traditional pattern," but today many synagogues say or sing part of the עֲמִידָה out loud together and do not have a repetition.

The Talmud teaches the history of the עֲמִידָה:

Each of these בְּרָכוֹת was originally sung by the angels when something important happened on earth.

Later the prophets gathered these songs into a collection of prayers.

After the Temple was destroyed by the Romans in 70 C.E., the Rabbis collected these prayers and organized them into a service to replace the sacrifices that took place in the Temple.

Once the Temple was the place that connected all Jews to each other and to God. Now, all Jews are connected by the path to God created by the בְּרָכוֹת in the עֲמִידָה.

In this unit you will learn:
• about the purpose of the עֲמִידָה
• about the parts of the עֲמִידָה
• the story of Ḥannah

9

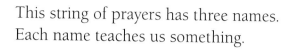

This string of prayers has three names.
Each name teaches us something.

עֲמִידָה means standing. This name reminds us that this prayer is said standing (in a whisper, with our feet together). This standing is a way of being like the angels, acting out the story of Ḥannah, and physically showing our connection to God. (We will learn all of these stories.)

• שְׁמוֹנֶה עֶשְׂרֵה means the eighteen. Originally the עֲמִידָה had eighteen בְּרָכוֹת. Today there are nineteen. One was added for the protection of Israel from enemies. The number eighteen teaches many different lessons about how to get close to God. Various rabbis have researched and found various things that come only eighteen times. They include: God's Name in the שְׁמַע; sentences that have Abraham, Isaac, and Jacob together in the Torah; and specific prayers that are said by individuals in the Torah. Finally, we learn that there are eighteen joints in the spine. Together these things teach that we should connect to God through prayer, the way our ancestors did. God supported them and God supports us just as our spine does.

הַתְּפִלָּה means The Prayer. Its root[פלל] has two different meanings. [פלל] can mean to check out. It means that one part of prayer is doing a self-check, finding out how we are doing as God's partner. Another meaning is to ask for. The תְּפִלָּה is the part of the service where we ask God for the things we need.

Rav Kook, the first Chief Rabbi of Israel, taught, The עֲמִידָה is where we learn what is really important in life. It teaches us the difference between the things we need and the things we just want. The עֲמִידָה is our time to ask God for the things we really need.

Question: What is the difference between really needing something and just wanting it? What things do we need that are not food, clothing, and shelter?

Can you see the three letters עמד in these words?

עַמּוּד   עֲמִידָה   עוֹמֵד

stand = עוֹמֵד

Amidah, standing = עֲמִידָה

page, column = עַמּוּד
pillar, lectern

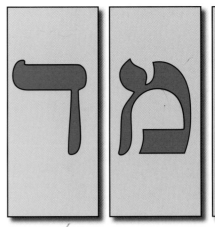

עֲמִידָה is one of the names for the "standing prayer."

Practice these words and circle all the words that contain the root עמד.

1. אֲבוֹתֵינוּ   ⟨עוֹמֵד⟩   תְּפִלָּה ⟨עוֹמְדִים⟩ ⟨יַעֲמְדוּ⟩   אִמוֹתֵינוּ

2. אֱלֹהֵינוּ ⟨עֲמִידָה⟩ הַגָּדוֹל   הַגִּבּוֹר ⟨עַמּוּד⟩ הַנּוֹרָא ⟨יַעֲמֹד⟩

Can you see the three letters פלל in these words?

תְּפִלָּה   לְהִתְפַּלֵּל   פִּלֵּל

Sometimes one of the ל letters falls out.

judged = פִּלֵּל

to pray = לְהִתְפַּלֵּל

prayer = תְּפִלָּה

הַתְּפִלָּה is one of the names for the "standing prayer."

Practice these phrases that contain the root פלל.

3. וַאֲנִי תְפִלָּתִי לְךָ יי עֵת רָצוֹן   וְקַבֵּל בְּרַחֲמִים וּבְרָצוֹן אֶת-תְּפִלָּתֵנוּ

4. בָּרוּךְ אַתָּה יי שׁוֹמֵעַ תְּפִלָּה   כִּי אֵל שׁוֹמֵעַ תְּפִלּוֹת וְתַחֲנוּנִים אָתָּה

11

Practice, Practice, Practice

Practice these עֲמִידָה words.

1. אֲבוֹתֵינוּ אִמּוֹתֵינוּ גִּבּוֹר מְחַיֶּה מֵתִים קָדוֹשׁ אַתָּה

2. וְנֶאֱמָן גְּבוּרוֹת יְשַׂמַּח מֹשֶׁה וְשָׁמְרוּ בְּנֵי יִשְׂרָאֵל

3. וֵאלֹהֵי שְׂפָתַי עֶלְיוֹן זָכְרֵנוּ בְּאַהֲבָה מְכַלְכֵּל חַיִּים

4. אָז בְּקוֹל מַשְׁמִיעִים תִּתְקַדַּשׁ יָמוּשׁ בְּעֵינֶיךָ מוֹדִים

5. חֲסָדִים תְּהִלָּתֶךָ לְהוֹשִׁיעַ אֱמוּנָתוֹ לְהַחֲיוֹת תִּתְגַּדַּל

6. בְּצֵאת הַלְלוּיָהּ נָגִילָה מִמְּקוֹמְךָ אֲסוּרִים וּמַצְמִיחַ

Practice these עֲמִידָה phrases.

7. אַתָּה קָדוֹשׁ וְשִׁמְךָ קָדוֹשׁ וּקְדוֹשִׁים בְּכָל־יוֹם יְהַלְלוּךָ סֶּלָה

8. בָּרוּךְ אַתָּה יי אֱלֹהֵינוּ וֵאלֹהֵי אֲבוֹתֵינוּ וְאִמּוֹתֵינוּ

9. יי יי אֵל רַחוּם וְחַנּוּן אֶרֶךְ אַפַּיִם וְרַב חֶסֶד וְאֶמֶת

10. אֱלֹהֵינוּ וֵאלֹהֵי אֲבוֹתֵינוּ רְצֵה בִמְנוּחָתֵנוּ קַדְּשֵׁנוּ בְּמִצְוֹתֶיךָ

11. מוֹדִים אֲנַחְנוּ לָךְ שָׁאַתָּה הוּא יי אֱלֹהֵינוּ וֵאלֹהֵי אֲבוֹתֵינוּ

12. סוֹמֵךְ נוֹפְלִים וְרוֹפֵא חוֹלִים וּמַתִּיר אֲסוּרִים וּמְקַיֵּם אֱמוּנָתוֹ

13. וְטוֹב בְּעֵינֶיךָ לְבָרֵךְ אֶת־עַמְּךָ יִשְׂרָאֵל בְּכָל־עֵת וּבְכָל־שָׁעָה בִּשְׁלוֹמֶךָ

Hannah's Prayer

annah lived in the time of the judges. This was after the time that Joshua led the Families-of-Israel back into the Land of Israel and before King David made them into a real nation.

Hannah had a problem. She had a husband named Elkanah, but he was not the problem. He loved her a lot. Elkanah had a second wife named Penninah. Penninah was part of the problem. She had children, while Hannah had none. Even though Penninah had given birth to his children, Hannah was still Elkanah's favorite wife. To get even, Penninah picked on Hannah a lot. She was good at making Hannah feel bad about not having children. Her feelings about not being a mother were Hannah's biggest problem.

The worst time for her was the one time a year when the whole family went to Shiloh. The Mishkan (Tablernacle) was stationed there, and the family would go there to celebrate. Elkanah would go and stand in line and bring back portions of the sacrifice for the whole family. He gave Hannah her own portion. He gave Penninah a whole stack of portions for her and her children. For Hannah the pile of portions was the scoreboard of her failure. She got only her single portion, and that made her feel alone. When Penninah got lots of portions, Hannah felt that made Penninah a success.

One of those nights in Shiloh Hannah went for a walk. She was wandering close to the Mishkan and praying to God. She was speaking very softly. Her lips were moving, but no one else could hear her words. Hannah was begging God for a child.

Eli was the High Priest. He ran the sacrifices and the Mishkan. He saw this woman wandering and talking to herself, close to the Mishkan, and he thought she was drunk. He yelled at her for not respecting a holy place. Hannah answered him, "I have not had one drop to drink. I am just a woman who is מָרַת נֶפֶשׁ." In most translations this will read "very sad" or "very bitter." But the Hebrew actually means "I have horseradish in my soul." Just like when you eat too much horseradish and your whole head turns red—it is too much for you—Hannah's sadness and hurt were too much for her. She explained that she had turned to God for help. Eli heard her and understood. He said, "May God answer your prayers." God did. Hannah gave birth to Samuel, who was a very famous judge and prophet.

The Rabbis studied her story and made her the model for the עֲמִידָה. We stand and whisper our prayers the way she stood and whispered her prayers. We try to have מָרַת נֶפֶשׁ (horseradish in our souls), needing what we pray for and knowing that only God can help us (*1 Samuel, Chapter 1; Brakhot 30b-31a*).

Questions

1. Why do you think that God answered Hannah's prayer and gave her the blessing for which she asked?
2. What made her a good choice for being the model of the way we should pray the עֲמִידָה?
3. How can knowing this story help you know where to point your heart when you stand to begin the עֲמִידָה?

14

The עֲמִידָה

Practice saying or singing these parts of the עֲמִידָה.

The weekday עֲמִידָה is made up of 19 בְּרָכוֹת.

Praise

The first three בְּרָכוֹת praise God. Here are a small piece of each of these:

1. בָּרוּךְ אַתָּה יי אֱלֹהֵינוּ וֵאלֹהֵי אֲבוֹתֵינוּ וְאִמוֹתֵינוּ...
בָּרוּךְ אַתָּה יי מָגֵן אַבְרָהָם וְעֶזְרַת שָׂרָה/וּפוֹקֵד שָׂרָה.

Blessed are You, ADONAI, our God and God of our fathers and mothers...
Blessed be You, ADONAI, the SHIELD of Abraham and the ONE-Who HELPS/REMEMBERS Sarah.

2. אַתָּה גִבּוֹר לְעוֹלָם אֲדֹנָי מְחַיֶּה מֵתִים/הַכֹּל אַתָּה...
בָּרוּךְ אַתָּה יי מְחַיֶּה מֵתִים/הַכֹּל.

You are mighty ADONAI, you give life to the dead/all. Blessed be You, ADONAI, the ONE Who-Gives-Life to the **dead/all**.

3. אַתָּה קָדוֹשׁ וְשִׁמְךָ קָדוֹשׁ וּקְדוֹשִׁים בְּכָל־יוֹם יְהַלְלוּךָ סֶּלָה...
בָּרוּךְ אַתָּה יי הָאֵל הַקָּדוֹשׁ.

You are HOLY and Your name is HOLY and... Blessed be You, ADONAI the HOLY God.

Petition

The next thirteen בְּרָכוֹת are a "shopping list" asking God for the things we need.

4. אַתָּה חוֹנֵן לְאָדָם דַּעַת...בָּרוּךְ אַתָּה יי חוֹנֵן הַדָּעַת.

You favor people with KNOWLEDGE... Blessed be You, ADONAI, The ONE-Who-Makes-a-GIFT of KNOWLEDGE.

5. הֲשִׁיבֵנוּ אָבִינוּ לְתוֹרָתֶךָ...בָּרוּךְ אַתָּה יי הָרוֹצֶה בִּתְשׁוּבָה.

RETURN us, Our Parent, to Your Torah... Blessed be You, ADONAI, The ONE-Who-WANTS REPENTENCE.

6. סְלַח לָנוּ אָבִינוּ כִּי חָטָאנוּ...בָּרוּךְ אַתָּה יי חַנּוּן הַמַּרְבֶּה לִסְלֹחַ.

FORGIVE us, Our Parent, because we miss the mark... Blessed be You, ADONAI, The ONE-Who-MULTIPLIES opportunities to be FORGIVEN.

7. רְאֵה נָא בְעָנְיֵנוּ וְרִיבָה רִיבֵנוּ וּגְאָלֵנוּ מְהֵרָה לְמַעַן שְׁמֶךָ...
בָּרוּךְ אַתָּה יי גּוֹאֵל יִשְׂרָאֵל.

See our suffering and make problems for those who cause us problems, and REDEEM us quickly... Blessed be You, ADONAI, The ONE-Who-REDEEMS Israel.

Over

8. רְפָאֵנוּ יי וְנֵרָפֵא...בָּרוּךְ אַתָּה יי רוֹפֵא חוֹלֵי עַמּוֹ יִשְׂרָאֵל.

HEAL us ADONAI and we will be HEALED... Blessed be You, ADONAI, The ONE-Who-HEALS the sick of Israel.

9. בָּרֵךְ עָלֵינוּ יי אֱלֹהֵינוּ אֶת-הַשָּׁנָה הַזֹּאת.....

בָּרוּךְ אַתָּה יי מְבָרֵךְ הַשָּׁנִים.

ADONAI, our God, MAKE THE YEAR A BLESSING FOR US... Blessed be You, ADONAI, The ONE-Who-BLESSES the YEARS.

10. תְּקַע בְּשׁוֹפָר גָּדוֹל לְחֵרוּתֵנוּ וְשָׂא נֵס לְקַבֵּץ גָּלְיוֹתֵינוּ....

בָּרוּךְ אַתָּה יי מְקַבֵּץ נִדְחֵי עַמּוֹ יִשְׂרָאֵל.

Sound the big SHOFAR for our FREEDOM and lift up a FLAG to signal the INGATHERING of the EXILES... Blessed be You, ADONAI, The ONE-Who-GATHERS the EXILES of Israel.

11. הָשִׁיבָה שׁוֹפְטֵינוּ כְּבָרִאשׁוֹנָה...בָּרוּךְ אַתָּה יי מֶלֶךְ אֹהֵב צְדָקָה וּמִשְׁפָּט.

Return our JUDGES... Blessed be You, ADONAI, The RULER-Who loves RIGHTEOUSNESS and JUSTICE.

12. וְלַמַּלְשִׁינִים אַל תְּהִי תִקְוָה...

בָּרוּךְ אַתָּה יי שֹׁבֵר אֹיְבִים וּמַכְנִיעַ זֵדִים.

And for the INFORMERS don't let there be hope... Blessed be You, ADONAI The ONE-Who-Shatters the ENEMIES and oppresses the WICKED.

Petition

13. עַל הַצַּדִּיקִים וְעַל הַחֲסִידִים...

בָּרוּךְ אַתָּה יי מִשְׁעָן וּמִבְטָח לַצַּדִּיקִים.

For the RIGHTEOUS and for the PIOUS... Blessed are You, ADONAI, The ONE-Who-SUPPORTS and the ONE-Who-is-the-TRUST of the RIGHTEOUS.

14. וְלִירוּשָׁלַיִם עִירְךָ בְּרַחֲמִים תָּשׁוּב...בָּרוּךְ אַתָּה יי בּוֹנֵה יְרוּשָׁלָיִם.

And to JERUSALEM Your City, RETURN in mercy... ... Blessed be You, ADONAI, The ONE-Who-BUILDS JERUSALEM.

15. אֶת-צֶמַח דָּוִד עַבְדְּךָ מְהֵרָה תַצְמִיחַ....

בָּרוּךְ אַתָּה יי מַצְמִיחַ קֶרֶן יְשׁוּעָה.

The SEED of DAVID, Your sevant, quickly PLANT, and the HORN of REDEMPTION lift up... Blessed be You, ADONAI, The ONE-Who-PLANTS the HORN of SALVATION.

16. שְׁמַע קוֹלֵנוּ יי אֱלֹהֵינוּ...בָּרוּךְ אַתָּה יי שׁוֹמֵעַ תְּפִלָּה.

HEAR our VOICE, ADONAI, our God... Blessed be You, ADONAI, The ONE-Who-HEARS prayers.

To Think About

1. Why is praise, petition, and thanksgiving a good way to organize these prayers?

2. Why do you think the middle בְּרָכוֹת are removed on שַׁבָּת?

3. How is the עֲמִידָה like the spine of the Jewish people?

The last three בְּרָכוֹת in the עֲמִידָה thank God for all the blessings we have received.

17. רְצֵה יי אֱלֹהֵינוּ בְּעַמְּךָ יִשְׂרָאֵל וּבִתְפִלָּתָם...
בָּרוּךְ אַתָּה יי הַמַּחֲזִיר שְׁכִינָתוֹ לְצִיּוֹן.

ADONAI, our God want YOUR PEOPLE ISRAEL and their PRAYERS... Blessed are You, ADONAI, The ONE-Who-RETURNS GOD'S NEIGHBORLY ASPECT to ZION.

18. מוֹדִים אֲנַחְנוּ לָךְ שָׁאַתָּה הוּא יי אֱלֹהֵינוּ...
בָּרוּךְ אַתָּה יי הַטּוֹב שִׁמְךָ וּלְךָ נָאֶה לְהוֹדוֹת.

We give THANKS TO YOU, ADONAI, our God... Blessed are You, ADONAI the good-ONE is Your NAME and it is beautiful to THANK YOU.

19. שִׂים שָׁלוֹם טוֹבָה וּבְרָכָה חֵן וָחֶסֶד וְרַחֲמִים...
בָּרוּךְ אַתָּה יי הַמְבָרֵךְ אֶת־עַמּוֹ יִשְׂרָאֵל בַּשָּׁלוֹם

Give PEACE, GOODNESS, BLESSINGS, NICENESS, LOVINGKINDNESS, and MERCY......
Blessed be You, ADONAI, The ONE-Who-BLESSES Israel with PEACE.

ON SHABBAT: The 13 בְּרָכוֹת of petition are removed and in their place comes a short blessing about Shabbat. Included is:

וְשָׁמְרוּ בְנֵי יִשְׂרָאֵל אֶת־הַשַּׁבָּת...בָּרוּךְ אַתָּה יי מְקַדֵּשׁ הַשַּׁבָּת.

The Families-of-Israel shall keep Shabbat... Praised are You, Adonai, the ONE-Who-makes-HOLY the Shabbat.

Find the connection between the first part of each prayer and the sentence with בָּרוּךְ אַתָּה יי at the end. Usually there is a word or a root that connects the beginning to the end.

Some Answers

Praise, Petition, and Thanksgiving: The midrash explains this three-part structure with this image. Imagine someone going before a ruler in order to make a request. It would not be good to start with a list of requests. Rather, the person would begin, "The world is better because of this ruler. The world is better because this ruler is a fair judge..." The entire audience would then join that person in praising the ruler. After that start would be the time for requests. The עֲמִידָה is set up in the same way, first praise, then requests (*Sifre, Deut.* 343).

The **praise** בְּרָכוֹת resemble a servant praising a boss. The **petition** בְּרָכוֹת resemble a servant who asks a boss for a favor. The **thanksgiving** בְּרָכוֹת resemble a servant who has gotten the favor for which he has asked (*Brakhot* 34a).

The middle בְּרָכוֹת **are removed on** שַׁבָּת: In order to make a "true petiton" one must feel a sense of sadness, hurt, and desperation. In a petition we are asking God to help us meet a need we cannot meet alone. (See the story of Ḥannah.) Shabbat is supposed to be a happy time, a celebration. Shabbat is not a time for us to dwell on the saddest parts of our life.

The Amidah as a Spine: We have already learned that one of the reasons that we have eighteen בְּרָכוֹת in the עֲמִידָה is to compare it to the spine.

How to Dance the עֲמִידָה

We begin the עֲמִידָה by standing up, facing Jerusalem, taking three steps forward, and then standing with our feet together. Some of the prayers we may sing together, but if we don't, they are said in a whisper, loud enough to be heard by your own ears but by no one else.

Each of these "dance steps" has us acting out a different story.

When we **stand up** we are like Abraham. Abraham was the first person to figure out that there was only one God. In the Talmud (*Brakhot* 26b) we learn that he invented the morning service. He got up every morning and stood before the God he knew was there.

When we **face Jerusalem** we are like King Solomon (*1 Kings* 8.44-48) creating a house where God can be our neighbor. When we face toward Jerusalem we are recreating our pilgrimage toward the Temple where sacrifices united all Jews. Now, three times a day, the עֲמִידָה creates the same connections.

When we take **three steps forward** we are like Moses. Moses went up Mount Sinai to come close to God. The Torah tells us that there was darkness, a cloud, and thick fog between Moses and the top of the mountain (*Deut.* 4.11). God was hidden, and Moses had to work to get close. The three steps are our darkness, cloud, and fog. They remind us that we, too, have to work to feel close to God. (Often people take three steps back in order to take three steps forward.)

The Baal Shem Tov explained these three steps by saying, When a child is learning to walk, a parent takes three steps back and stands with open arms, giving the child room to learn. Like a parent, God takes three steps back from us, to give us the room we need. To begin the עֲמִידָה we take those three steps back to God.

When we **whisper** we are like Hannah. Hannah was a woman who needed God's help. She whispered when she prayed, and God answered her. In the Talmud we are taught, We whisper to remind ourselves that God is always close. We have no need to yell (*Sotah* 32b; *Brakhot* 31a).

When we **stand with our feet together** we are like angels. In the Bible we learn that angels who are close to God's throne stand with their feet together (*Ezekiel* 1.7). When we ask God for the things we need, we stand like one of those angels.

Who or what do you feel like when you stand and begin the עֲמִידָה?

עֲצֹר!

18

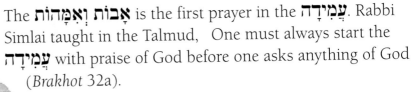

אָבוֹת וְאִמָּהוֹת

The אָבוֹת וְאִמָּהוֹת is the first prayer in the עֲמִידָה. Rabbi Simlai taught in the Talmud, One must always start the עֲמִידָה with praise of God before one asks anything of God (*Brakhot* 32a).

The אָבוֹת וְאִמָּהוֹת is the first of three praise בְּרָכוֹת that begin the עֲמִידָה.

The big idea of this prayer is זְכוּת אָבוֹת (the merit of our ancestors). This means that we ask God to take care of us because our ancestors were good people who had good relationships with God.

The Rabbis who organized the סִדּוּר explained their choice of the אָבוֹת וְאִמָּהוֹת as the first prayer because of a Torah story about Moses.

When Israel sinned with the Golden Calf, God was ready to destroy them. Moses stood and prayed to the Holy One to try to change God's mind. None of his prayers worked until he said: Do it for the sake of Abraham, Isaac, and Israel your servants. It was those words that got God to forgive Israel. Therefore, we begin our עֲמִידָה with that same reminder to God (*Mehilta, Bo* 13.3; *Shabbat* 30a).

Originally, this prayer was just about the אָבוֹת, the fathers, אַבְרָהָם, יִצְחָק, and יַעֲקֹב. Like many things in Judaism, it was man centered. Today many synagogues have added the אִמָּהוֹת, the mothers, שָׂרָה, רִבְקָה, לֵאָה and רָחֵל. This came as part of a growing understanding that all of us need women's stories, too.

Nahmanides, a famous biblical commentator, taught: This prayer only works if we remind ourselves of our ancestors' lives and make a commitment to take their values and make them part of our lives. Why would doing that be a good thing?

In this unit you will learn:

• about the אָבוֹת וְאִמָּהוֹת

• roots יש ע זכר חסד and the ה that means "The."

• 6 Major stories

אָבוֹת וְאִמָּהוֹת

Blessed be You, ADONAI	בָּרוּךְ אַתָּה יי 1.
our God and God of our FATHERS & our MOTHERS	אֱלֹהֵינוּ וֵאלֹהֵי אֲבוֹתֵינוּ וְאִמּוֹתֵינוּ. 2.
God of ABRAHAM	אֱלֹהֵי אַבְרָהָם 3.
God of ISAAC	אֱלֹהֵי יִצְחָק 4.
and God of JACOB.	וֵאלֹהֵי יַעֲקֹב. 5.
God of SARAH	אֱלֹהֵי שָׂרָה 6.
God of REBEKKAH	אֱלֹהֵי רִבְקָה 7.
God of LEAH	אֱלֹהֵי לֵאָה 8.
and God of RACHEL	וֵאלֹהֵי רָחֵל. 9.
The GOD, The GREAT One, The HERO, THE AWESOME One	הָאֵל הַגָּדוֹל הַגִּבּוֹר וְהַנּוֹרָא 10.
God on High	אֵל עֶלְיוֹן 11.
The ONE-Who-NURSES with GOOD KINDNESS	גּוֹמֵל חֲסָדִים טוֹבִים 12.
and the ONE-Who-OWNS everything	וְקוֹנֵה הַכֹּל 13.
and the ONE-Who-REMEMBERS the kindness of the Parents,	וְזוֹכֵר חַסְדֵי אָבוֹת וְאִמָּהוֹת 14.
and brings a REDEMEER/REDEMPTION to their children's children	וּמֵבִיא גוֹאֵל/גְּאוּלָה לִבְנֵי בְנֵיהֶם 15.
for the sake of God's NAME.	לְמַעַן שְׁמוֹ בְּאַהֲבָה. 16.
RULER, HELPER—and SAVIOR and PROTECTOR	מֶלֶךְ עוֹזֵר וּמוֹשִׁיעַ וּמָגֵן. 17.
Blessed be You, ADONAI	בָּרוּךְ אַתָּה יי 18.
The ONE-Who-PROTECTS Abraham	מָגֵן אַבְרָהָם 19.
and The ONE-Who HELPS Sarah/REMEMBERS Sarah.	וְעֶזְרַת שָׂרָה/וּפוֹקֵד שָׂרָה. 20.

Why does this prayer begin with אֱלֹהֵינוּ and then say אֱלֹהֵי אֲבוֹתֵינוּ? To teach us that one should not just believe in God because one's family did, but because of one's own search and one's own discovery (*Otzar ha-T'fillot*).

Why does the prayer repeat אֱלֹהֵי for each mother and father? It is probably based on Exodus 3.15, which says, This is what you should say to the Families-of-Israel: The Eternal, God of your Ancestors, the God of Abraham, the God of Isaac, and the God of Jacob, has sent me to you. We can learn from here that each of the אָבוֹת had a different relationship with God. Each had a different faith (*Rabbi Zev Ya'avetz*).

our God = אֱלֹהֵינוּ

the God of = אֱלֹהֵי

God = אֵל

God = אֱלֹהִים

your God = אֱלֹהֶיךָ

The Hebrew word אֱלֹהִים has three different meanings. (1) It means judges, including human judges. (2) It means gods. And (3) it means The One and Only God.

One big question that gets asked is, Why use a word that means gods to stand for God? Here is the best answer. יי is God's name. אֱלֹהִים is the job (God) that יי does. It says that one God does the job everyone else thought it took lots of gods to do.

Practice these phrases that have God in them, and circle the word for God in each.

1. בָּרוּךְ אַתָּה יי הָאֵל הַקָּדוֹשׁ

2. בָּרוּךְ אַתָּה יי אֱלֹהֵינוּ וֵאלֹהֵי אֲבוֹתֵינוּ וְאִמוֹתֵינוּ

3. יי יי אֵל רַחוּם וְחַנּוּן אֶרֶךְ אַפַּיִם וְרַב חֶסֶד וֶאֱמֶת

4. אֵל מָלֵא רַחֲמִים שׁוֹכֵן בַּמְּרוֹמִים

5. אֱלֹהֵי שָׂרָה אֱלֹהֵי רִבְקָה אֱלֹהֵי לֵאָה וֵאלֹהֵי רָחֵל

6. הָאֵל הַגָּדוֹל הַגִּבּוֹר וְהַנּוֹרָא אֵל עֶלְיוֹן, גּוֹמֵל חֲסָדִים טוֹבִים

7. אֵל אָדוֹן עַל כָּל-הַמַּעֲשִׂים בָּרוּךְ וּמְבֹרָךְ בְּפִי כָּל-נְשָׁמָה

8. מִי כָמֹכָה בָּאֵלִם יי מִי כָּמֹכָה נֶאְדָּר בַּקֹּדֶשׁ נוֹרָא תְהִלֹּת עֹשֵׂה פֶלֶא

בָּרוּךְ אַתָּה יי אֱלֹהֵינוּ וֵאלֹהֵי אֲבוֹתֵינוּ וְאִמּוֹתֵינוּ

blessed are you   are god   god   god and   the   god of our fathers   and our mothers

אֱלֹהֵי אַבְרָהָם אֱלֹהֵי יִצְחָק וֵאלֹהֵי יַעֲקֹב

the   god   of   Aberham   the   god of   Israle   and the   god of Jacob

אֱלֹהֵי שָׂרָה אֱלֹהֵי רִבְקָה אֱלֹהֵי לֵאָה וֵאלֹהֵי רָחֵל

the god of   Sarah the   god of Reabeca   the god Leah   and the god of Rach

בָּרוּךְ

Your teacher will help you with your translation.

Word Parts

our = נוּ

and = וְ

of = יְ

your = ךָ

Words

God = אֵל

אַתָּה

אָב

אֵם

אַבְרָהָם

יִצְחָק

עֲצֹר!

Choreography

We bend our knees and bow on the opening and closing of this בְּרָכָה.

Sefer Abudarham, a major commentary on the סִדּוּר, teaches that we are supposed to bend like a lulav, separating each of the joints in our spine.

Bowing symbolizes a sense of humility. Arrogance keeps people from connecting. Egotism creates distance between you and God (*Brakhot* 34a).

The שֻׁלְחָן עָרוּךְ (*Orekh Hayyim* 113.7) teaches we should bend our whole body as if we were falling down, but stand up straight before we reach God's name (יי). This reminds us that God is the One who keeps us from falling.

What is your best reason for bowing at the beginning of the אָבוֹת וְאִמָהוֹת?

יַעֲקֹב

שָׂרָה

רִבְקָה

לֵאָה

רָחֵל

back to page 20 and read the אָבוֹת וְאִמָּהוֹת before you work on this page.

Find the Ancestor in Each Verse

Practice these Torah phrases. Circle the ancestor in each phrase.

1. וְהָיָה שִׁמְךָ אַבְרָהָם כִּי אַב־הֲמוֹן גּוֹיִם נְתַתִּיךָ

2. וַתִּצְחַק שָׂרָה בְּקִרְבָּה לֵאמֹר אַחֲרֵי בְלֹתִי הָיְתָה־לִּי עֶדְנָה וַאדֹנִי זָקֵן

3. וַיֹּאמֶר קַח־נָא אֶת־בִּנְךָ אֶת־יְחִידְךָ אֲשֶׁר אָהַבְתָּ אֶת־יִצְחָק

4. וַתִּשָּׂא רִבְקָה אֶת־עֵינֶיהָ וַתֵּרֶא אֶת־יִצְחָק וַתִּפֹּל מֵעַל הַגָּמָל

5. וַיִּגַּשׁ יַעֲקֹב אֶל־יִצְחָק אָבִיו וַיֹּאמֶר הַקֹּל קוֹל יַעֲקֹב וְהַיָּדַיִם יְדֵי עֵשָׂו

6. וַיְהִי בָעֶרֶב וַיִּקַּח אֶת־לֵאָה בִתּוֹ וַיָּבֵא אֹתָהּ אֵלָיו וַיָּבֹא אֵלֶיהָ

7. וַיִּזְכֹּר אֱלֹהִים אֶת־רָחֵל וַיִּשְׁמַע אֵלֶיהָ אֱלֹהִים וַיִּפְתַּח אֶת־רַחְמָהּ

The "The"

ה is a Hebrew prefix that means "the". When you add ה to the word אֵל, it becomes הָאֵל "the God."

Look at these words. Circle those with the prefix ה.

1. הַגִּבּוֹר   וֵאלֹהֵי   הַגָּדוֹל   חֲסָדִים   הַמֵּתִים

2. הָעוֹלָם   חַסְדֵי   הַזָּן   אֶת   הַכֹּל   וְאִמָּהוֹת

גָּדוֹל

Your teacher will help you with your translation.

הָאֵל הַגָּדוֹל הַגִּבּוֹר וְהַנּוֹרָא אֵל עֶלְיוֹן

My best guess at the meaning of this line is:

_____

_____

גִּבּוֹר

עֶלְיוֹן

Word Parts

the = הַ/הָ

and = וְ

Words

God = אֵל

awesome = נוֹרָא

A Moses Moment

In the Torah Moses says to the Families-of-Israel, "Cut away the thickening from around your heart and do not keep your necks stiff anymore...for the Eternal your God is...great, mighty, and awesome...your God whom you are to hold in awe and whom you are to serve..." This prayer is based on that teaching. When we say it we are having a Moses moment.

What does it mean to "cut away the thickening from our hearts and to not keep our necks stiff"? How does knowing that God is "great, mighty, and awesome" help us do that?

Researching the אָבוֹת וְאִמָּהוֹת

Connecting to Our Ancestors

Nahmanides, a famous Bible commentator, taught, We are allowed to use זְכוּת אָבוֹת (the good connections built by our ancestors with God) to our own advantage if we (1) love the things for which they stood and (2) are committed to following their example.

We have also learned that this prayer says אֱלֹהֵי (God of) individually for each of the אָבוֹת and אִמָּהוֹת because each had his or her own unique relationship with God.

Studying the אָבוֹת וְאִמָּהוֹת

To follow the spiritual path that Nahmanides recommends, we need to learn about our ancestors. We need to know their example if we are to follow it. Working alone or with a team you are going to research one of the matriarchs or patriarchs.

Your teacher will give you the time and resources you can use, but you can start with the biographies on page 26-27.

Name of the Ancestor:_____

1. One important moment in the life of my ancestor was when:

   _____
   _____

2. The thing that was most special about my ancestor's relationship with God was that:

   _____
   _____

3. One moment in my life that is similar to my ancestor's important moment was when:

   _____
   _____

4. One lesson I can take from my ancestor's example into my own life is:

   _____
   _____

God and the אָבוֹת וְאִמָּהוֹת

גִּבּוֹר—Isaac

Isaac's big moment in the Torah is a very difficult and scary story (*Gen. 22*). God told Abraham to bring Isaac up a mountain as a sacrifice. Abraham followed orders and brought him up as a sacrifice. God stopped the whole thing before Isaac beccame a sacrifice. The midrash praises Isaac for not rebelling and going along with this test. They said that he had גְּבוּרָה (self-control and self-discipline). In the Torah we learn a secret from Isaac. God is called פַּחַד יִצְחָק (the Fear of Isaac). Sometimes God can scare us.

נוֹרָא—Jacob

Jacob had two major experiences of God in his life. When he left home he had a dream of angels going up and down on a ladder. He said, How awesome is this place (*Gen. 27.17*). Later, Jacob wrestled with a stranger who changed his name to יִשְׂרָאֵל (The One-Who-wrestles-with-God). In between, he started a huge family that grew into the twelve tribes, the Nation of Israel. The rabbis said that Jacob served God through תִּפְאֶרֶת (truth and beauty). In the Bible we learn that God was אֲבִיר יַעֲקֹב (The Mighty One of Jacob).

גָּדוֹל—Abraham

We learn from the midrash that Abraham was the first person to believe in one God. He discovered God through looking at the world. Abraham then spent his life welcoming strangers and treating all people as if they were created in God's image. He was big on doing חֶסֶד (acts of loving kindness). He also spent his time spreading the knowledge that there was only One God. In the Bible we are told that Abraham was God's friend (*Isaiah 41.8*) and that God was the מָגֵם אַבְרָהָם (shield of Abraham) (*Gen. 15.1*).

The אָבוֹת וְאִמָּהוֹת quotes Moses and calls God הַגָּדוֹל, הַגִּבּוֹר, הַנּוֹרָא. In the Zohar we are taught that אַבְרָהָם experienced God as הַגָּדוֹל, that יִצְחָק experienced God as הַגִּבּוֹר, and that יַעֲקֹב knew God as הַנּוֹרָא.

passive bride, she saw to it that Jacob and not Esau became the future of the Jewish people. Rabbi Beth Singer writes, "Rebekkah is clear-sighted, smart, humble, courageous, loyal, loving, and above all else, spiritually connected and clear regarding her life's purpose...She invites each of us to open our eyes to God's presence, to pray for awareness that our lives have meaning, and to direct our actions to...be God's partners in the continual work of creation" (*The Women's Torah Commentary*).

Leah & Rachel

Leah was the older sister, the one with weak eyes, the quiet one. Jacob was tricked into marrying her, but she was the one who gave him many children. Rachel was the beautiful sister, the one everyone noticed. She is the one that Jacob first met and loved.

Leah and Rachel together teach us a very important lesson sisterhood. Even though they were in competition, even though sharing meant that they would each have less, these two women took care of each other. We learn in the midrash (*Lam. R.* 24) that Rachel helped Leah trick Jacob rather than revealing the plot. We learn in another midrash that Leah prayed for Rachel to have a child, even though it would mean competition for her children (*Midrash ha-Gadol*). In the book of Ruth we are told, "May the Eternal make the woman who is coming into your house like Rachel and Leah, who together built up the house of Israel."

Because we come from the generation that has added the אִמָּהוֹת to the עֲמִידָה, we have work to do to learn about them and discover the examples they set for us.

Sarah

Sarah was Abraham's partner and a prophetess. She shared the work of welcoming strangers and spreading the knowledge of the One God. She was the mother of souls (*Gen. R.* 12.8). Sarah's big thing was laughter. When God first told her that she was to have a child, she laughed in a bitter, angry way. She did not believe it was possible for an old woman to give birth (*Gen.* 18.12). When Sarah gave birth to Isaac, her laughter changed. It became the laughter of joy. Sarah gave God credit, saying, "God has made laughter for me" (*Gen.* 21.6). Sarah let God help her heal her sadness and bitterness.

Rebekkah

Rebekkah was picked to be Isaac's bride because she shared many values with Abraham. Hospitality and care for others were big parts of her life. When she herself was unable to have a child, she turned to God in sincere prayer. When twins were fighting in her womb she asked, "If this is so, why am I?" Rather than just being a

Go back to page 20 and practice the אָבוֹת וְאִמָהוֹת before you work on this page.

Can you see the three letters חסד in these words?

חֶסֶד חַסְדֵי חֲסָדִים

kindness = חֶסֶד

kindness of = חַסְדֵי

acts of kindness = גְמִילוּת חֲסָדִים

Practice these words and circle all the words that contain the root חסד.

1. גְמִילוּת חֲסָדִים אֲבוֹתֵינוּ אֵל עֶלְיוֹן נוֹרָא חֶסֶד

2. זוֹכֵר חַסְדֵי אָבוֹת אִמָהוֹת גָדוֹל גִבּוֹר הַכֹּל

We've studied this root before.

remembers = זוֹכֵר

remember us = זָכְרֵנוּ

memory, rembrance = זִכָּרוֹן

Practice these phrases and circle all the words that contain the root זכר.

3. זֵכֶר לִיצִיאַת מִצְרַיִם לְמַעַן תִזְכְּרוּ וַעֲשִׂיתֶם אֶת כָּל-מִצְוֹתָי

every thing to remember *remember*

4. בָּרוּךְ אַתָּה יי זוֹכֵר הַבְּרִית זָכְרֵנוּ לְחַיִים מֶלֶךְ חָפֵץ בַּחַיִים

אֵם   אָב   זוֹכֵר   חֶסֶד

Word Parts
and = וְ

Your teacher will help you with your translation.

וְזוֹכֵר חַסְדֵי אָבוֹת וְאִמָּהוֹת

My best guess at the meaning of this line is:

_____

_____

Practice, Practice and More Practice

Practice these phrases from the אָבוֹת וְאִמָּהוֹת.

1. אֱלֹהֵי לֵאָה וֵאלֹהֵי רָחֵל   גּוֹמֵל חֲסָדִים טוֹבִים וְקוֹנֵה הַכֹּל

2. מֶלֶךְ עוֹזֵר וּמוֹשִׁיעַ וּמָגֵן   הָאֵל הַגָּדוֹל הַגִּבּוֹר הַנּוֹרָא אֵל עֶלְיוֹן

3. לְמַעַן שְׁמוֹ בְּאַהֲבָה   בָּרוּךְ אַתָּה יי אֱלֹהֵינוּ וֵאלֹהֵי אֲבוֹתֵינוּ

4. אֱלֹהֵי אַבְרָהָם אֱלֹהֵי יִצְחָק וֵאלֹהֵי יַעֲקֹב אֱלֹהֵי שָׂרָה אֱלֹהֵי רִבְקָה

5. וְזוֹכֵר חַסְדֵי אָבוֹת וְאִמָּהוֹת וּמֵבִיא גוֹאֵל לִבְנֵי בְנֵיהֶם

6. בָּרוּךְ אַתָּה יי מָגֵן אַבְרָהָם וּפוֹקֵד שָׂרָה

7. בָּרוּךְ אַתָּה יי מָגֵן אַבְרָהָם וְעֶזְרַת שָׂרָה

29

The Power of a Biography

One day a stranger walked into the yeshivah and sat and listened to the lecture given by the Rosh Yeshivah, the head of the school. After the lesson, the stranger, dressed like a successful businessman, stood in the back. After the students had gone he walked up to the Rosh Yeshivah and smiled. The rabbi asked, Do I know you?

The stranger responded, Don't you recognize me? I was your _hevruta_, your study partner, when we were in yeshivah thirty years ago.

The Rosh Yeshivah looked at him closely, turning back the years. He then said, Of course I remember you. You changed my life. You were the one who taught me how to learn. You gave me the tools to become who I am today.

The old friend suddenly looked sad. The Rosh Yeshivah asked, What's wrong? The friend answered, I was just thinking about how I wasted my own potential. I had a real talent for learning and teaching, and yet I never followed through. Why did you grow into a great rabbi while I just drifted away?

The rabbi answered, Do you remember that biography of the Vilna Gaon that was on the reading room table? When you read it, your face was shining and you said, 'That man was just amazing.' When I read it I said to myself, 'I am going to be as like him as I can manage.' That, my friend, was the only difference.

Rabbi Yitzchak Sender told this story and taught, זְכוּת אָבוֹת is not just acknowledging the greatness of our ancestors but taking up the challenge they offer and attempting to emulate them.

(_The Commentator's Siddur_)

In modern Hebrew there is a word פְּרוֹטֶקְצִיָּה "protectzia." It is slang and comes from the English word "protection." When you need something done and you call in a favor based on a connection (especially a family connection) it is called "protectzia." It is easy to think that starting the עֲמִידָה with the אָבוֹת וְאִמָּהוֹת is an attempt to do the same thing. This story teaches another understanding of זְכוּת אָבוֹת.

עֲצֹר!

Questions

1. Explain the difference between these two friends.
2. How can a biography or a story change your life?
3. How can knowing this story help you know where to point your heart when you say the אָבוֹת וְאִמָּהוֹת?

Go back to p... and practice the אָבוֹת וְאִמָּהוֹת before you work on this page.

Can you see the root יש"ע in these words?

וּמוֹשִׁיעַ   לְהוֹשִׁיעַ   יְשׁוּעָה

Hebrew builds words out of three-letter roots.

Sometimes the י drops out.

and saved = וּמוֹשִׁיעַ

to save = לְהוֹשִׁיעַ

salvation = יְשׁוּעָה

Salvation comes from "save." It is the Jewish idea (that Christians adopted also) that God has, and will save us.

Practice these phrases and circle all the words that contain the root יש"ע.

1. מֶלֶךְ עוֹזֵר וּמוֹשִׁיעַ וּמָגֵן. בָּרוּךְ אַתָּה יי מָגֵן אַבְרָהָם וְעֶזְרַת שָׂרָה

2. אַתָּה גִבּוֹר לְעוֹלָם אֲדֹנָי מְחַיֵּה מֵתִים אַתָּה רַב לְהוֹשִׁיעַ

3. צוּר חַיֵּינוּ מָגֵן יִשְׁעֵנוּ אַתָּה הוּא לְדוֹר וָדוֹר

4. אַשְׁרֵי אָדָם בֹּטֵחַ בָּךְ יי הוֹשִׁיעָה הַמֶּלֶךְ יַעֲנֵנוּ בְיוֹם קָרְאֵנוּ

5. לְחַיִּים וּלְשָׁלוֹם, לְשָׁשׂוֹן וּלְשִׂמְחָה לִישׁוּעָה וּלְנֶחָמָה וְנֹאמַר אָמֵן

6. וַאֲנִי תְפִלָּתִי לְךָ יי עֵת רָצוֹן אֱלֹהִים בְּרָב חַסְדֶּךָ עֲנֵנִי בֶּאֱמֶת יִשְׁעֶךָ

7. כִּי בְשֵׁם קָדְשְׁךָ הַגָּדוֹל וְהַנּוֹרָא בָּטָחְנוּ נָגִילָה וְנִשְׂמְחָה בִּישׁוּעָתֶךָ

8. כִּי אֵל פּוֹעֵל יְשׁוּעוֹת אָתָּה וּבָנוּ בָחַרְתָּ מִכָּל עַם וְלָשׁוֹן

Your teacher will help you with your translation.

מֶלֶךְ

מָגֵן

Word Parts

and = וְ

Words

help = עוֹזֵר

save = מוֹשִׁיעַ

מֶלֶךְ עוֹזֵר וּמוֹשִׁיעַ וּמָגֵן.

My best guess at the meaning of this line is:

_____

_____

Abraham Was a Hero

A war was going on in Canaan. It had nothing to do with Abraham. Four local kings were fighting five other local kings. Abraham (who was still Abram) was camped in the trees at Mamre when a refugee from the war staggered into camp. The refugee told him that Abraham's nephew Lot, who lived in Sodom, had been taken prisoner. The four kings had raided Sodom and Gomorrah, robbed all the wealth, and then run away. Abraham gathered an army from the people in his camp. He chased the four kings into the north of Canaan. His army caught them and defeated them. Abraham rescued Lot and gathered up all of the possessions that had been stolen. He returned everything to the original owners. He kept nothing for himself. He gave nothing to his army. Melchizedek, king of Salem, threw a party. He gave Abraham (still Abram) a blessing. He said, Blessed be Abram of אֵל עֶלְיוֹן, Creator of heaven and earth. Abraham then blessed God with words that would later become part of the Psalms: You, God, are a shield about me...I have no fear of the many forces that surround me (Ps. 3.4-7). At that moment the angels in heaven started to sing, בָּרוּךְ אַתָּה יי מָגֵן אַבְרָהָם (Gen. 14.; P.R.E. 27).

Questions

1. What are the things we learn about Abraham that make him into a hero?
2. What connections do we find between this story and the אָבוֹת וְאִמָהוֹת?
3. How can knowing this story help you know where to point your heart when you say the אָבוֹת אִמָהוֹת?

32

Shield of Abraham

This is a midrash. Once Abram (who would grow up to become Abraham) discovered that there was only one God, he could not stop spreading the news. His father, Tera_h_, was an idol maker. Abram worked hard to convince his father's customers that the idols they wanted to buy were of no use.

A powerful man came in and asked for a powerful idol. Abram asked, How old are you? The man answered, I have lived seventy years. Abram asked him, Then why do you want to bow down before a piece of stone that was carved a few days ago? The man left.

One day Abram smashed all the idols in his father's store except for one. He put a stick in that idol's hand and told his father, This idol got in a fight with the other idols and broke them. Tera_h_ yelled at his own son, Are you making fun of me? They are stone they cannot

do anything! Abram answered, Father, learn from your own words.

Tera<u>h</u> took his son and handed him over to Nimrod, the wicked local king. Nimrod challenged him, Don't you know that I am god, the Ruler of the Universe. Abram said to him, Then tomorrow please make the sun rise in the west and set in the east. Nimrod stared at him with anger. Abram then said to him, You are no god. You are just the son of Cush. You could not keep your father from dying and eventually you will die, too.

Nimrod had Abram taken away. He was put to work as a slave. The project Abram was working on was the Tower of Babel. This was Nimrod's attempt to reach heaven. Workers on the tower were trained to care more about the bricks than about other workers. Abram started a slave revolt. He taught everyone that there was only One God, that people should care about each other, and that no tower could reach God. Eventually God mixed up the languages of the workers and Abram escaped.

Abram went back home and continued teaching people that Nimrod was not god, because there was only One God. Nimrod had him arrested again. He was taken into the center of the city, tied hand and foot, and placed on a huge bonfire. The fire burned and burned but Abram was protected. Nimrod grabbed his sword and his shield. The shield was a triangle with the point at the bottom. It stood for Everything comes to me. Abram called for a sword and shield. His shield was also a triangle. Its point was at the top and meant everything comes from God. The two of them began to fight on the bonfire. It was hot. At one point they banged their shields together and the shields fused. Abram pulled back and he now had a shield with six points. Nimrod fled and Abram was safe. That six-pointed shield was first מָגֵן אַבְרָהָם. Only later did it become מָגֵן דָּוִד. At that moment the angels sang בָּרוּךְ אַתָּה יי מָגֵן אַבְרָהָם *(Gen. R. 38.13; P.R.E. 24; Shlomo Carlebach and other sources).*

Questions

1. What things do we learn about Abram from this story? When have you been like him?
2. What do we learn about מָגֵן אַבְרָהָם from this story?
3. How can knowing this story help you know where to point your heart when you say the אָבוֹת אִמָּהוֹת?

34

בָּרוּךְ

אַתָּה

מָגֵן

אַבְרָהָם

שָׂרָה

 Go back to page 20 and read the אָבוֹת וְאִמָּהוֹת before you work on this page.

בָּרוּךְ אַתָּה יי מָגֵן אַבְרָהָם וְעֶזְרַת שָׂרָה/וּפוֹקֵד שָׂרָה.

Your teacher will help you with your translation.

My best guess at the meaning of this line is:

_____

_____

To Talk About

In the midrash a rabbi named Resh Lakish teaches, "The אָבוֹת and אִמָּהוֹת are chariots (*Gen. R.* 47.6)." This idea is explained by saying that our prayers can ride on them and reach God. How do you think this works?

God Remembers Sarah

Resh Lakish also taught (in the days when this prayer only included the אָבוֹת) that while the prayer begins with all of the אָבוֹת, it ends with only אַבְרָהָם to fulfill a promise that God made. When Abraham agreed to leave home and follow God, God made him five promises. The first was "You shall be a blessing" (*Gen.* 12.12). מָגֵן אַבְרָהָם is his blessing (*Pesaḥim* 117b).

When the אִמָּהוֹת were added to this blessing Sarah got to share the final slot. Some סִדּוּרִים talk about עֶזְרַת שָׂרָה (the God who helped Sarah). Many now use פּוֹקֵד שָׂרָה (the God who remembered Sarah). This is based on Genesis 21.1. It says, "The Eternal visited/remembered Sarah as God had said, and the Eternal did for Sarah as God had promised." The same root פקד is also used to tell what God did for the Jewish people when they were slaves in Egypt. "And the people believed when they heard that the Eternal had remembered/visited the people of Israel and had seen their affliction, they bowed their heads and worshiped" (*Ex.* 4.31).

What is special about a God who is פּוֹקֵד שָׂרָה?

Word Parts

and = וְ,וּ

Words

help = עֶזְרַה

remember = פּוֹקֵד

Sarah's Tent

Sarah had a tent of her own. Every time that the family made camp, Sarah's tent was set up first. Abraham taught men about the One God. Sarah was the women's teacher. Abraham's tent had doors on all four sides so that everyone who was looking for hospitality could easily find their way in. Sarah's tent was where Shabbat was created. Every week Sarah baked _hallah_. Every week Sarah lighted Shabbat candles. The smell of the _hallah_ lasted from week to week. It was always in the tent. The Shabbat lights burned from one Shabbat until the next set were kindled. The tent always smelled of _hallah_. It was always a place of light.

The _Shekhinah_ is the part of God that gets close to people. It is the part that can be our neighbor. God was comfortable with Sarah and her tent. God liked the smell and the light and the peace of Shabbat. The _Shekhinah_ would come down in a cloud and rest on Sarah's tent.

When Sarah died, her tent grew dark; the smell of _hallah_ began to fade. Isaac was sad. He refused to see anyone. Abraham sent his servant back to Padam Aram, the old country, to find a wife for Isaac. The servant picked Rebekkah. When Rebekkah rode into camp, she and Isaac saw each other and fell immediately in love. He took her into his mother's tent. She baked _hallah_ and then lit Shabbat candles. The tent smelled of _hallah_ again. The tent was filled with light again. The _Shekhinah_ came back. Isaac finally found comfort after his mother's death.

Years passed. God was hiding in the seventh heaven and crying. Israel had rejected the commandments. They had made a golden calf. All God's dreams were shattered like the tablets. God needed a way to start over. God needed a new beginning. Then God remembered Sarah's tent. God told Moses to have Israel built a tent and to place within it twelve loaves of braided bread and a light that never went out. The tent would always smell like _hallah_. It would always be a place of light (this was the Mishkan Tabernacle). God promised that God would come down and be a neighbor just as God had at Sarah's tent (_Gen. R._ 60.16).

Questions
1. What does this story teach us about Sarah?
2. When have you been like her?
3. How can knowing this story help you to know where to point your heart when you say the אָבוֹת וְאִמָּהוֹת?

עֲצֹר!

37

Sarah's Tents

The words to the אָבוֹת וְאִמָהוֹת are on Sarah's tents.
Connect the phrases to each other to find the full prayer.

מֶלֶךְ עוֹזֵר
וּמוֹשִׁיעַ וּמָגֵן.

9

בָּרוּךְ אַתָּה יי

4

אֱלֹהֵי אַבְרָהָם
אֱלֹהֵי יִצְחָק
וֵאלֹהֵי יַעֲקֹב.

3

אֱלֹהֵי שָׂרָה
אֱלֹהֵי רִבְקָה
אֱלֹהֵי לֵאָה
וֵאלֹהֵי רָחֵל.

4

בָּרוּךְ אַתָּה יי
מָגֵן אַבְרָהָם
וּפוֹקֵד שָׂרָה

10

אֱלֹהֵינוּ וֵאלֹהֵי
אֲבוֹתֵינוּ וְאִמּוֹתֵינוּ

2

הָאֵל הַגָּדוֹל
הַגִּבּוֹר וְהַנּוֹרָא
אֵל עֶלְיוֹן

5

וּמֵבִיא גְאֻלָּה
לִבְנֵי בְנֵיהֶם לְמַעַן
שְׁמוֹ בְּאַהֲבָה.

9

וּמֵבִיא גּוֹאֵל
לִבְנֵי בְנֵיהֶם לְמַעַן
שְׁמוֹ בְּאַהֲבָה.

8

גּוֹמֵל חֲסָדִים
טוֹבִים
וְקוֹנֵה הַכֹּל

6

וְזוֹכֵר חַסְדֵי
אָבוֹת וְאִמָהוֹת

7

בָּרוּךְ אַתָּה יי
מָגֵן אַבְרָהָם
וְעֶזְרַת שָׂרָה

10

38

The Missing Mother (A Bonus Story)

Abraham's mother was called Amat'la-i, the daughter of Karnibo, but you can't find her story in the Torah. You have to look for her in the Talmud and the midrash.

Nimrod was the wicked king who built the tower of Babel. Like all wicked kings he wanted people to believe that he was a god. Nimrod learned from an astrologer that soon a male child would be born who would grow up and teach everyone that Nimrod was not a god. That did not make Nimrod happy. He ordered the midwives of his empire to make sure that all male babies died. At the same time he offered a prize for every girl that was born. Nimrod built a huge palace and made all of the pregnant women in his realm live there. He pretended to take care of them, but this gave him a chance to make sure that no boys survived.

Amat'la-i was married to Tera<u>h</u>, the idol maker. He was a member of Nimrod's court. Amat'la-i hid the fact that she was pregnant. She knew that if Tera<u>h</u> knew, he would turn her in. When it was time for her to give birth she went out to the wilderness. Abram (who would become Abraham) was born in a cave. His mother blessed him with three blessings: "May God be with you. May God never fail you. May God never leave you." Then she left him.

Here is where the miracles start. Baby Abram sucked his thumb, and out came milk. This milk was amazing food. Ten days after his birth Abram was big enough and strong enough to stand up and walk out of the cave. He looked at the world and the way that nature works. He became the first person to figure out that One God had created everything. He prayed to that One God, saying, "I believe in you." Then, for the first time, he heard God's voice saying, "And I believe in you."

Amat'la-i felt sick about having abandoned her child. She ran back to the cave and found it empty. While she was sitting at its entrance sobbing, a child, not a newborn, came up to her and said, "Why are you crying?" She explained, and he said, "Mother, don't you recognize me?" She hugged him, and he explained to her about the One God. Abraham's mother, the one who risked her life to give him life, became his first student (Based on Louis Ginzberg, *The Legends of the Jews*).

Questions

1. In what ways was Amat'la-i a great role model? All Jews (even Jews-by-choice) are children of Abraham. That makes her your "Grandmother." In what ways would you like to be like her?

2. The hard thing about this story is knowing that Amat'la-i left her newborn baby alone in a cave. How can you understand that?

3. How can knowing the story of Abraham's mother help you point your heart when you pray the אָבוֹת וְאִמָּהוֹת?

Reviewing אָבוֹת וְאִמָּהוֹת

Some things to know about אָבוֹת וְאִמָּהוֹת

The אָבוֹת וְאִמָּהוֹת is the first of three praise-בְּרָכוֹת that begin the עֲמִידָה.

The idea at the heart of this בְּרָכָה is זְכוּת אָבוֹת (the merit of the ancestors). It not only means that we ask God to listen to our prayer because of our family heritage but that we promise to live up to the examples set by them.

The אָבוֹת וְאִמָּהוֹת is rooted in Moses' plea to God to forgive the Families-of-Israel for the Golden Calf, and in stories of God protecting Abraham. But, while those two stories are the origins of the prayer every story we know about the אָבוֹת and אִמָּהוֹת add to our understandings of it.

Originally, this prayer was just the אָבוֹת. The adding of the אִמָּהוֹת is a sign of one major growth in Jewish understanding.

Language Learning

Among the words and word parts we worked with in this unit are:

Roots: ע שׁ י and חסד, זכר

Words: אַב רָחֵל לֵאָה רִבְקָה שָׂרָה יַעֲקֹב יִצְחָק אַבְרָהָם

מָגֵן גִּבּוֹר גָּדוֹל אֵם

Body Language: We bow at the beginning and ending בָּרוּךְ of this בְּרָכָה.

The Ending of this Prayer captures its central message:

בָּרוּךְ אַתָּה יי מָגֵן אַבְרָהָם וְעֶזְרַת שָׂרָה/וּפוֹקֵד שָׂרָה.

Blessed be You, ADONAI, The ONE-Who-PROTECTS Abraham

and the ONE-Who HELPS Sarah/REMEMBERS Sarah.

גְּבוּרוֹת

The גְּבוּרוֹת is:

The second of the three praise בְּרָכוֹת that begin the עֲמִידָה.

A prayer that the Talmud names two different ways.

Called the גְּבוּרוֹת (the power prayer) (*Megillah* 17b). That makes it a prayer that talks about God's power through describing some of the good things that God does for people.

It is called מְחַיֵּה הַמֵּתִים (The One Who-Gives-Life-to-the-Dead) (*Brakhot* 33a). It is a prayer that traditionally centers on the idea that God is stronger than death.

The גְּבוּרוֹת is a place where some modern Jews have changed the סִדּוּר. In a number of סִדּוּרִים the phrase מְחַיֵּה הַמֵּתִים is replaced by מְחַיֵּה הַכֹּל (The One Who-Gives-Life-to-All), or מְחַיֵּה כָּל חַי (The One Who-Gives-and-Renews Life).

This בְּרָכָה is built around the language of Psalm 146. There we are told that God:

keeps faith forever	arranges justice
feeds the hungry	sets prisoners free
lifts up the fallen	

In the *Inyyun ha-Tefillah*, a commentary on the סִדּוּר, we are taught, This prayer shows that while people often use their strength to defeat and conquer others, God uses power in the opposite way.

In the same way that the אָבוֹת וְאִמָּהוֹת, the first prayer in the עֲמִידָה, tells the story of אַבְרָהָם and שָׂרָה and their experiences of God, the גְּבוּרוֹת grows out of stories of יִצְחָק רִבְקָה and (and a יוֹסֵף story, too).

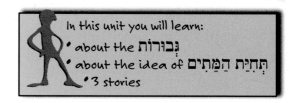

In this unit you will learn:
- about the גְּבוּרוֹת
- about the idea of תְּחִיַת הַמֵּתִים
- 3 stories

גְּבוּרוֹת (מֵתִים)

You are a HERO forever, my Master:	אַתָּה גִּבּוֹר לְעוֹלָם אֲדֹנָי	1.
You give LIFE to the dead	מְחַיֵּה מֵתִים אַתָּה	2.
You are GREAT to bring SALVATION.	רַב לְהוֹשִׁיעַ.	3.
The ONE-Who-Returns the wind and Makes the rain come down.	מַשִּׁיב הָרוּחַ וּמוֹרִיד הַגֶּשֶׁם.	
The One-Who-Makes the dew come down.	וּמוֹרִיד הַטָּל.	
Cultivating LIFE in kindness	מְכַלְכֵּל חַיִּים בְּחֶסֶד	4.
Giving LIFE to the dead with much mercy.	מְחַיֵּה מֵתִים בְּרַחֲמִים רַבִּים.	5.
The ONE-Who-LIFTS-UP the fallen	סוֹמֵךְ נוֹפְלִים	6.
and HEALS the sick	וְרוֹפֵא חוֹלִים	7.
and FREES prisoners	וּמַתִּיר אֲסוּרִים	8.
and ESTABLISHES faith	וּמְקַיֵּם אֱמוּנָתוֹ	9.
with those who sleep in the dust.	לִישֵׁנֵי עָפָר.	10.
Who is like You, Master of Strength?	מִי כָמוֹךָ בַּעַל גְּבוּרוֹת?	11.
And Who has Your Image?	וּמִי דוֹמֶה לָּךְ?	12.
RULER of DEATH and LIFE	מֶלֶךְ מֵמִית וּמְחַיֶּה	13.
and the ONE-Who-Plants SALVATION.	וּמַצְמִיחַ יְשׁוּעָה.	14.
And You are faithful to give LIFE to the dead.	וְנֶאֱמָן אַתָּה לְהַחֲיוֹת מֵתִים.	15.
Blessed be You, ADONAI, The One-Who-Gives LIFE to the dead.	בָּרוּךְ אַתָּה יי מְחַיֵּה הַמֵּתִים.	16.

The Prayer for Rain

From the last day of Sukkot until the first day of Pesah we add the words מַשִּׁיב הָרוּחַ וּמוֹרִיד הַגֶּשֶׁם to the גְּבוּרוֹת. Some Jews add the phrase מוֹרִיד הַטָּל during the times that מַשִּׁיב הָרוּחַ is not said.

In the Tur (*O.H.* 114), a legal code, the connection between the גְּבוּרוֹת and the prayer for rain is explained, "Just as the resurrection of the dead will bring the dead back to life, so the rain brings the world back to life."

In the Talmud (*Ta'anit* 2a) Rabbi Abahu said, "Rain is a bigger miracle than resurrection of the dead because the rain falls for everyone, where only the good will be resurrected."

The Origins of the גְּבוּרוֹת

Most of the prayers in the סִדּוּר were assembled out of biblical images. Each time we find a source it gives us another story to connect:

continued on page 43

42

גְּבוּרוֹת (הַכֹּל)

1. You are a HERO forever, my Master:	1. אַתָּה גִבּוֹר לְעוֹלָם אֲדֹנָי
2. You give LIFE to all	2. מְחַיֶּה הַכֹּל אַתָּה
3. You are GREAT to bring SALVATION.	3. רַב לְהוֹשִׁיעַ.
The ONE-Who-Returns the wind and Makes the rain come down.	מַשִּׁיב הָרוּחַ וּמוֹרִיד הַגָּשֶׁם.
The One-Who-Makes the dew come down.	וּמוֹרִיד הַטָּל.
4. Cultivating LIFE in kindness	4. מְכַלְכֵּל חַיִּים בְּחֶסֶד
5. Giving LIFE to all with much mercy.	5. מְחַיֶּה הַכֹּל בְּרַחֲמִים רַבִּים.
6. The ONE-Who-LIFTS-UP the fallen	6. סוֹמֵךְ נוֹפְלִים
7. and HEALS the sick	7. וְרוֹפֵא חוֹלִים
8. and FREES prisoners	8. וּמַתִּיר אֲסוּרִים
9. and ESTABLISHES faith	9. וּמְקַיֵּם אֱמוּנָתוֹ
10. with those who sleep in the dust.	10. לִישֵׁנֵי עָפָר.
11. Who is like You, Master of Strength?	11. מִי כָמוֹךָ בַּעַל גְּבוּרוֹת?
12. And Who has Your Image?	12. וּמִי דוֹמֶה לָּךְ?
13. RULER of DEATH and LIFE	13. מֶלֶךְ מֵמִית וּמְחַיֶּה
14. and the ONE-Who-Plants SALVATION.	14. וּמַצְמִיחַ יְשׁוּעָה.
15. And You are faithful to give LIFE to all.	15. וְנֶאֱמָן אַתָּה לְהַחֲיוֹת הַכֹּל.
16. Blessed be You, ADONAI, The One-Who-Gives LIFE to all.	16. בָּרוּךְ אַתָּה יי מְחַיֶּה הַכֹּל.

אַתָּה גִבּוֹר (You are **mighty**): Moses, asking forgiveness for the Golden Calf, called God נוֹרָא and גִבּוֹר, גָּדוֹל.

מְכַלְכֵּל חַיִּים בְּחֶסֶד (**cultivating/sustaining life** in kindness): We learn that Yosef did the same thing (with the root כלכל). "Yosef sustained his father and his family with food..." (*Gen.* 47.12).

סוֹמֵךְ נוֹפְלִים וְרוֹפֵא חוֹלִים וּמַתִּיר אֲסוּרִים (**Lifts up the fallen**...and establishes **faith**): In Psalm 146 we read about God, "(God) keeps faith forever, secures justice for those who have been wronged, gives food to the hungry. The Eternal sets prisoners free...the Eternal lifts up those who are fallen."

לִישֵׁנֵי עָפָר: In the book of Daniel (12.2) we find this prayer: "(May) many of those who sleep in the dust awake some to eternal life, some to punishment...." It speaks of judgment after death.

To Talk About: What can each of these stories teach us about the גְּבוּרוֹת?

1. וּמְקַיֵּם אֱמוּנָתוֹ לִישֵׁנֵי עָפָר.

2. מִי כָמוֹךָ בַּעַל גְּבוּרוֹת?　　וּמִי דוֹמֶה לָּךְ?

3. מֶלֶךְ מֵמִית וּמְחַיֶּה　　וּמַצְמִיחַ יְשׁוּעָה

4. סוֹמֵךְ נוֹפְלִים　　וְרוֹפֵא חוֹלִים　　וּמַתִּיר אֲסוּרִים

5. מְכַלְכֵּל חַיִּים בְּחֶסֶד　　מְחַיֶּה הַכֹּל בְּרַחֲמִים רַבִּים.

6. אַתָּה גִּבּוֹר לְעוֹלָם אֲדֹנָי　　מְחַיֶּה מֵתִים אַתָּה רַב לְהוֹשִׁיעַ.

7. וְנֶאֱמָן אַתָּה לְהַחֲיוֹת הַכֹּל　　בָּרוּךְ אַתָּה יי מְחַיֶּה הַמֵּתִים

Phrase Detective

Look at these four phrases from the גְּבוּרוֹת.
What can you find that all four phrases have in common?

8. אַתָּה גִּבּוֹר לְעוֹלָם אֲדֹנָי מְחַיֶּה מֵתִים אַתָּה רַב לְהוֹשִׁיעַ

9. מְכַלְכֵּל חַיִּים בְּחֶסֶד מְחַיֶּה מֵתִים בְּרַחֲמִים רַבִּים

10. מֶלֶךְ מֵמִית וּמְחַיֶּה וּמַצְמִיחַ יְשׁוּעָה

11. וְנֶאֱמָן אַתָּה לְהַחֲיוֹת מֵתִים. בָּרוּךְ אַתָּה יי מְחַיֶּה הַמֵּתִים

עֲצֹר!

Circle all the words built out of the root חי, and underline words built out of the root מֵת. We'll talk about what these words mean in the next lesson.

44

Make your best guess at the meaning and then compare these two versions of the first line of the גְּבוּרוֹת.

Your teacher will help you with your translation.

אַתָּה

גִּבּוֹר

עוֹלָם

Words

אֲדֹנָי = Adonai

חַי = life

מֵת = dead

רַב = great

הוֹשִׁיעַ = salvation

Word Parts

הַ = the   לְ = to

אַתָּה גִּבּוֹר לְעוֹלָם אֲדֹנָי מְחַיֶּה מֵתִים אַתָּה רַב לְהוֹשִׁיעַ.

_____

_____

אַתָּה גִּבּוֹר לְעוֹלָם אֲדֹנָי מְחַיֶּה הַכֹּל אַתָּה רַב לְהוֹשִׁיעַ.

_____

_____

Background on the Two Versions

תְּחִיַּת הַמֵּתִים (Resurrection of the Dead) is a belief that at some time in the future God will regather our bodies from the soil and place our souls back in them, giving us a second chance to live.

1. Maimonides was a famous Jewish philosopher who wrote a list of thirteen things that every Jew was supposed to believe. Number thirteen has to do with the phrase מְחַיֶּה הַמֵּתִים giving life to the dead. I believe with complete faith that there will be a resurrection of the dead whenever the Creator wishes it...For Your salvation, Eternal, do I wait.

2. In 1869 a conference of Reform rabbis voted on a resolution and decided The belief in bodily resurrection has no religious foundation and the doctrine of immortality refers to the afterexistence of the soul alone. The Reform movement adopted מְחַיֶּה הַכֹּל giving life to all. Some services in recent Reform סִדּוּרִים have gone back to the original.

3. The Conservative Movement has left the words unchanged but often suggest different understandings. In a book called *Higher and Higher*, Steven M. Brown provides a list of alternative understandings: People live on in the memories of others. People's good works live on after them. The soul is resurrected and comes back in another body. People can be revived spiritually so life takes on new meaning. People recuperate after severe illness. Someone pronounced dead can be revived by C.P.R.

Ideas of the Afterlife

Gehenna

Jewish Ideas About the Afterlife

There are many different Jewish ideas of what happens after you die. Among them are: • The good that people do lives on. • People live on in memories. • The soul returns to God. • People's souls are reborn as another person (reincarnation). • There is a place like heaven called the Garden of Eden. • There is a place called *Gehenna* where bad people stay. • All good people will have their souls returned to their bodies, and they will live again.

The Rabbinic Idea of the Afterlife

In the Talmud there is a discussion of life after death. The one clear thing we learn in this discussion is that "God is stronger than death." This means that there is some kind of life after this life. It is called עוֹלָם הַבָּא, "the world to come." The Talmud makes it clear that Jews are supposed to believe that (1) God is fair, and (2) there is an afterlife (*Sanhedrin* 90b).

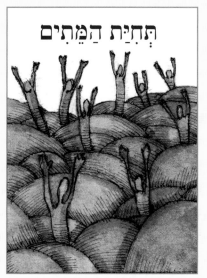

תְּחִיַּת הַמֵּתִים

Maimonides Tells the Story

Maimonides was a Jewish philosopher who lived in the Middle Ages. He gathered together Jewish traditions and told the story of the afterlife this way: After we die we are judged. Everyone goes to a place called *Gehenom* (or *Gehenna*) for usually no more than eleven months. Here God creates special opportunities for us to change and remove our worst tendencies. Very bad people stay in *Gehenom* forever, but most people go from there to the Garden of Eden (the Jewish version of heaven). When the Messiah comes, everyone who is in the Garden of Eden will be given the chance to live again. God will regather their bodies from the soil and place their souls back in them. This is called "resurrection of the dead." At this point, all of the good people will join with the Messiah and create the Messianic Era. The גְּבוּרוֹת celebrates this idea.

Gan Eden

Questions

There are many different Jewish ideas of what happens after you die.
1. Do you think that God is fair? Does God reward good people? Does God punish bad people?
2. Do you believe that God is stronger than death? What do you think happens after people die?
3. Which way do they read the גְּבוּרוֹת in your shul? (Is it מְחַיֶּה כָּל חַי or מְחַיֶּה הַכֹּל or מְחַיֶּה הַמֵּתִים?) What do the words your synagogue uses mean to you?

This is the way that one midrash retells the hardest story in the Torah.

God told Abraham to bring his son up "as an offering." Abraham tried some delaying tactics but they did not work.

He got up the next morning and saddled a donkey. The donkey was one of the miraculous things that God created in the last hour before the first Shabbat. This was the same donkey that Moses would use to take his wife and sons to Egypt. This was also the donkey that the Messiah will use to ride into Jerusalem.

Three days later they reached the mountain. They saw a pillar of fire rising from the mountain top a clear indication that the שְׁכִינָה, the neighborly part of God, was waiting there. They went up to the top of the mountain. God showed them a place where an altar had been built. It was where Cain and Abel had offered their sacrifices. It was where Noah and his family had offered sacrifices. Abraham rebuilt this altar. Later Solomon would build the Temple here. Later the Jewish People would build an altar on this spot, offer sacrifices, and ask to be forgiven.

Isaac said to his father, Please bind me hand and foot so that I do not flinch. Help me to follow the command to 'Honor your father.' God watched as Abraham was binding with all his heart and Isaac was bound with all his heart. The angels cried.

Abraham picked up the knife to kill his son. He touched the blade to Isaac's neck, and Isaac's soul fled. He was as good as dead. When the angels cried to Abraham, Lay not your hands upon the boy, Isaac's soul returned. He stood up and said, בָּרוּךְ אַתָּה יי מְחַיֵּה הַמֵּתִים. He said it not only about himself, but because he now understood that all people will have an afterlife.

Abraham sacrificed a ram on this altar and not his son. This ram was another one of the miraculous things created in the last hour before the first Shabbat. God turned the ram into a promise for a better future. Its ashes were used to mark the altar in the Temple. Its tendons would become the strings on King David's harp. Its skin would become Elijah's belt. Its horns became the *shofrot* that would announce the coming of the Messiah. The angels sang, בָּרוּךְ אַתָּה יי מְחַיֵּה הַמֵּתִים (*Pirke de Rabbi Eliezer* 31).

Questions

1. What did Isaac learn about God in this story?
2. How is this a story about תְּחִיַּת הַמֵּתִים?
3. How were the things made out of the ram signs of a better future?
4. How does this story help you know where to point your heart when you say the גְּבוּרוֹת?
5. If you belong to a synagogue that says מְחַיֵּה הַכֹּל, what can you learn about the גְּבוּרוֹת from this story?

עֲצֹר!

Go back to page 42-43 and read the גְבוּרוֹת before you work on this page.

יָשֵׁן   אָסוּר   חוֹלָה   רוֹפֵא   נוֹפֵל   סוֹמֵךְ

עָפָר

Words

free = מַתִּיר

establish = מְקַיֵּם

God's = אֱמוּנָתוֹ
faith

Your teacher will help you with your translation.

סוֹמֵךְ נוֹפְלִים וְרוֹפֵא חוֹלִים וּמַתִּיר אֲסוּרִים
וּמְקַיֵּם אֱמוּנָתוֹ לִישֵׁנֵי עָפָר

My best guess at the meaning of this part of the prayer is:

_____

_____

_____

_____

To Talk About

This בְּרָכָה lists some of the mighty things that God does: סוֹמֵךְ נוֹפְלִים, רוֹפֵא חוֹלִים, מַתִּיר אֲסוּרִים. These are all acts of גְּמִילוּת חֲסָדִים, deeds of loving kindess. The Talmud makes it clear that God does acts of גְּמִילוּת חֲסָדִים. Rabbi Simlai taught that the Torah begins and ends with גְּמִילוּת חֲסָדִים. It begins with God clothing the naked (Adam and Eve). It ends with God burying the dead (Moses) (*Sotah* 14b).

A story about Rebekkah shows that people can do the same. The midrash describes what Eliezer saw when he realized that she was the perfect bride for Isaac.

Eliezer saw a beautiful woman coming toward the well with a jug on her shoulder. She first stopped beside a crying child. The child had cut his foot on a sharp stone. She washed and bound the wound and told the child, Do not worry--this will soon heal. Then a half-blind woman came to the well to draw water. Rebekkah helped her carry the full pitcher of water home. When Rebekkah returned, Eliezer asked her to draw a little water for him.

Questions

1. What is the connection between God doing גְּמִילוּת חֲסָדִים and our doing גְּמִילוּת חֲסָדִים?
2. How can knowing these stories help us to point our hearts when we say the גְּבוּרוֹת?

Being Like God

In the Torah we are told that God created people בְּצֶלֶם אֱלֹהִים, in God's image. The rabbis of the Talmud make it clear that בְּצֶלֶם אֱלֹהִים is a way of acting, not a way of looking. God does not have hands or feet, eyes or a nose. But God does act in holy ways. Our potential is to act in the same kinds of ways that God does.

List three kinds of things we can do that match the things that God did.

What God Did.

What Can We Do?

1. God clothed Eve and Adam.

1._____
2._____
3._____

2. God visited Abraham when he was sick.

1._____
2._____
3._____

3. God heard Rebekkah when she cried out in need.

1._____
2._____
3._____

4. God fed Israel with manna when they were in the wilderness.

1._____
2._____
3._____

5. God gave Esther the strength to save the Jewish people.

1._____
2._____
3._____

6. God buried Moses.

1._____
2._____
3._____

Joseph the Tzadik

This story began with a father who favored one son over his other sons. Joseph, the favorite son, had dreams in which everyone bowed down to him. He was a kid who said me all the time. His brothers hated him for his dreams and for his special treatment.

One day, Jacob, their father, asked Joseph to go out to the pasture where the other brothers were watching the sheep. Joseph happily agreed. Maybe he didn't realize how much his brothers hated him. Maybe he didn't believe that anything bad could happen to him. Or maybe he just wanted to make his father happy. Whatever the reason, it was a trip that changed Joseph's life and his whole family's life.

Joseph's brothers captured him, threw him in a pit, told his father that he was dead, and sold him as a slave. Joseph wound up in Potiphar's house in Egypt. There Joseph became responsible. He cared about doing a good job. Joseph became a very successful head of Potiphar's household. The problem came when Potiphar's wife wanted to cheat on her husband with Joseph. They could have gotten away with it. But Joseph refused her saying, I have to be loyal to my master. The midrash says, He was ready to cheat but he saw his father's face.

Even though he said, No, Joseph wound up in jail. There he made a point of learning the language of everyone else in jail. The Torah makes a point of telling us God was with Joseph in jail. The midrash explains that Joseph lived with the knowledge that there was one God who demanded that people act with justice and kindness. Joseph became a leader in jail, too.

In jail Joseph explained some dreams. This got him the chance to explain Pharaoh's dreams. These dreams wound up meaning Seven years of plenty and then seven years of famine. Joseph wound up in charge of Egypt, and everyone loved him. They bowed down to him, just like in his childhood dreams.

When the famine came, Joseph made sure that there was food for everyone no favoritism. There was food for every Egyptian and food for strangers from other countries who came in need. Joseph could have charged oodles of money for the food, but he was fair and just in his pricing. The midrash tells us that he personally went and spoke to everyone who needed food in their own language using the languages he learned in jail.

When his brothers came down to Egypt Joseph had the power to get even with them. Instead of revenge, he did two things. First, he helped them understand what they had done that was wrong. This understanding was a gift. Then he made sure that his family had food, safety, and a good place to live. He forgave and helped them. In the tradition, Joseph, the kid who started out saying, me all the time was called יוֹסֵף הַצַּדִּיק, Joseph the Righteous Person (*Various midrashim*).

Questions
1. Why did the Rabbis of the Talmud think that Joseph was a צַדִּיק?
2. How did living with the knowledge that "God was with him" effect Joseph?
3. How can knowing the story of the kid who started out saying "me" all the time who turned in to יוֹסֵף הַצַּדִּיק help us to know where to point our hearts when we say the גְּבוּרוֹת?

Reviewing the גְּבוּרוֹת

Some things to know about the גְּבוּרוֹת:

It is the second of three praise בְּרָכוֹת that begin the עֲמִידָה.

Its central idea is that God is powerful. In the traditional version of this prayer תְּחִיַּת הַמֵּתִים (resurrection of the dead) is the primary example of God's power. The Reform and Reconstructionist movements usually replaces this image.

This בְּרָכָה carries an insertion for rain between Sukkot and Pesaḥ.

This בְּרָכָה is rooted in the stories of Isaac, Rebekkah and Joseph.

Language Learning
Among the words we worked with in this unit are:

Words:

 עָפָר יָשֵׁן אָסוּר חוֹלֶה רוֹפֵא נָפַל סוֹמֵךְ גִּבּוֹר

The Heart of the Prayer:

This prayer is big on telling us of the wonderful things that God does. At its heart we learn סוֹמֵךְ נוֹפְלִים וְרוֹפֵא חוֹלִים וּמַתִּיר אֲסוּרִים וּמְקַיֵּם אֱמוּנָתוֹ לִישֵׁנֵי עָפָר.

קְדוּשָׁה

The קְדוּשָׁה is understood to be the angels' prayer. For some Jews, angels are very real. For other Jews angels are a metaphor a way of describing a special state of holiness, a special sense of closeness to God.

The קְדוּשָׁה is built out of stories about Isaiah, Ezekiel, and Jacob.

The קְדוּשָׁה is:

the third praise בְּרָכָה that begins the עֲמִידָה.

said silently in some congregations and then sometimes repeated aloud. In other settings it is only said aloud by the congregation.

a dialogue, a back-and-forth singing or reading, between the congregation and the service leader.

a prayer about holiness.

There is a מִצְוָה called קִדּוּשׁ הַשֵּׁם. It means making God's name holy, and that means giving God a great reputation. Sometimes קִדּוּשׁ הַשֵּׁם means martyrdom. That is dying for a good cause because God's rules and God's values are sometimes worth giving up one's life for. But קִדּוּשׁ הַשֵּׁם can also mean living in such a way that God becomes real and holy to other people through your actions.

We learn in the Torah that we are supposed to be holy because God is holy (*Lev.* 19.2) and that the Jewish people are supposed to be a holy nation (*Ex.* 19.6). The Zohar makes it even clearer when it teaches, We fill the earth with holiness through doing מִצְוֹת. How can doing מִצְוֹת fill the world with holiness?

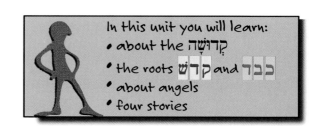

In this unit you will learn:
• about the קְדוּשָׁה
• the roots קדשׁ and כבד
• about angels
• four stories

53

קְדוּשָׁה

You are HOLY and Your NAME is HOLY	אַתָּה קָדוֹשׁ וְשִׁמְךָ קָדוֹשׁ	1.
and HOLINESS comes in praising You everyday. Selah.	וּקְדוֹשִׁים בְּכָל־יוֹם יְהַלְלוּךָ סֶּלָה.	2.
Blessed are You, ADONAI, The God, The HOLY (One).	בָּרוּךְ אַתָּה יי הָאֵל הַקָּדוֹשׁ.	3.

Let us make Your NAME HOLY in the Cosmos	נְקַדֵּשׁ אֶת שִׁמְךָ בָּעוֹלָם	5.
Just as they make it HOLY in the Heavens of the Heights—	כְּשֵׁם שֶׁמַּקְדִּישִׁים אוֹתוֹ בִּשְׁמֵי מָרוֹם	6.
As it is written by the hand of Your Prophet	כַּכָּתוּב עַל יַד נְבִיאֶךָ	7.
"And they called, one to the other, and said:	וְקָרָא זֶה אֶל זֶה וְאָמַר:	8.
HOLY, HOLY, HOLY is ADONAI of Hosts,	קָדוֹשׁ קָדוֹשׁ קָדוֹשׁ יי צְבָאוֹת	9.
all the world is full of God's HONOR."	מְלֹא כָל־הָאָרֶץ כְּבוֹדוֹ.	10.
Then in a voice, NOISY, BIG, KIND and STRONG	אָז בְּקוֹל רַעַשׁ גָּדוֹל אַדִּיר וְחָזָק	11.
they make their voices heard	מַשְׁמִיעִים קוֹל	12.
lifted up toward the seraphim	מִתְנַשְּׂאִים לְעֻמַּת שְׂרָפִים	13.
those facing the seraphim say, "BARUKH."	לְעֻמָּתָם בָּרוּךְ יֹאמֵרוּ.	14.
Blessed be ADONAI's honor from God's Place.	בָּרוּךְ כְּבוֹד יי מִמְּקוֹמוֹ.	15.
From Your Place, our Ruler	מִמְּקוֹמְךָ מַלְכֵּנוּ	16.
Appear to us and Rule over us	תוֹפִיעַ וְתִמְלוֹךְ עָלֵינוּ	17.
because we wait for You.	כִּי מְחַכִּים אֲנַחְנוּ לָךְ.	18.
When will You rule in Zion?	מָתַי תִּמְלוֹךְ בְּצִיּוֹן.	19.
Soon? In our days? Forever and ever come. Be our neighbor.	בְּקָרוֹב בְּיָמֵינוּ לְעוֹלָם וָעֶד תִּשְׁכּוֹן.	20.

Be made Great and be made HOLY	תִּתְגַּדַּל וְתִתְקַדַּשׁ	.21
inside Jerusalem Your city	בְּתוֹךְ יְרוּשָׁלַיִם עִירְךָ	.22
from generation to generation and from eternity to eternity.	לְדוֹר וָדוֹר וּלְנֵצַח נְצָחִים.	.23
And let our eyes see it—	וְעֵינֵינוּ תִרְאֶינָה	.24
Your Kingdom as it is said in the songs of Your strength	מַלְכוּתֶךָ כַּדָּבָר הָאָמוּר בְּשִׁירֵי עֻזֶּךָ	.25
written by the hand of David	עַל יְדֵי דָוִד	.26
the Annointed One of Your Righteousness.	מְשִׁיחַ צִדְקֶךָ.	.27
ADONAI, Rule forever, You are the God of Zion	יִמְלֹךְ יי לְעוֹלָם אֱלֹהַיִךְ צִיּוֹן	.28
from generation to generation. Hallelujah.	לְדֹר וָדֹר הַלְלוּיָהּ.	.29
From generation to generation we will tell of Your greatness	לְדוֹר וָדוֹר נַגִּיד גָּדְלֶךָ	.30
and from eternity to eternity Your holiness we make HOLY	וּלְנֵצַח נְצָחִים קְדֻשָּׁתְךָ נַקְדִּישׁ.	.31
and Your Praise, Our God, doesn't stop flowing from our mouths	וְשִׁבְחֲךָ אֱלֹהֵינוּ מִפִּינוּ לֹא יָמוּשׁ	.32
forever and ever.	לְעוֹלָם וָעֶד.	.33
Because You are The God, The Ruler, The Great One	כִּי אֵל מֶלֶךְ גָּדוֹל	.34
and The Holy One.	וְקָדוֹשׁ אָתָּה.	.35
Blessed are You, ADONAI	בָּרוּךְ אַתָּה יי	.36
The God, The HOLY One.	הָאֵל הַקָּדוֹשׁ.	.37

The עֲמִידָה begins with three בְּרָכוֹת: the אָבוֹת, the גְּבוּרוֹת, and the קְדוּשָׁה. These prayers all praise God and each teaches us about a different experience of God.

Moses called God three things: גָּדוֹל, גִּבּוֹר, and נוֹרָא. The גְּבוּרוֹת is connected to the idea that God is נוֹרָא (awesome). Solomon Schechter discovered that in ancient versions of the קְדוּשָׁה we are told that God's name is נוֹרָא. The אָבוֹת talked about God being גָּדוֹל, and the גְּבוּרוֹת called God גִּבּוֹר (Sefer ha-Eshkol, Shibolei ha-Leket, Reuven Kimmelman).

The קְדוּשָׁה is also connected to Jacob. It is about his ability to see אֱמֶת (the truth). The אָבוֹת was connected to אַבְרָהָם and שָׂרָה, the גְּבוּרוֹת to יִצְחָק and רִבְקָה (Sefer ha-Eshkol, Shibolei ha-Leket).

Can you see the three letters קדש in these words?

קָדוֹש מְקַדֵּש קִדְּשָׁנוּ

Hebrew builds words out of three-letter roots.

Holy = קָדוֹש

makes Holy = מְקַדֵּש

make us Holy = קִדְּשָׁנוּ

Practice these phrases and circle all the words that contain the root קדש.

1. בָּרוּךְ אַתָּה יי הָאֵל הַקָּדוֹש   אֲשֶׁר קִדְּשָׁנוּ בְּמִצְוֹתָיו וְצִוָּנוּ

2. בָּרוּךְ אַתָּה יי מְקַדֵּש הַשַּׁבָּת   וּבְדִבְרֵי קָדְשְׁךָ כָּתוּב לֵאמֹר

3. קָדוֹש קָדוֹש קָדוֹש יי צְבָאוֹת   מְלֹא כָל־הָאָרֶץ כְּבוֹדוֹ

4. אַתָּה קָדוֹש וְשִׁמְךָ קָדוֹש   וּקְדוֹשִׁים בְּכָל־יוֹם יְהַלְלוּךָ סֶּלָה

5. נְקַדֵּש אֶת־שִׁמְךָ בָּעוֹלָם כְּשֵׁם שֶׁמַּקְדִּישִׁים אוֹתוֹ בִּשְׁמֵי מָרוֹם

6. תִּתְגַּדַּל וְתִתְקַדַּש בְּתוֹךְ יְרוּשָׁלַיִם עִירְךָ לְדוֹר וָדוֹר וּלְנֵצַח נְצָחִים

7. נַעֲרִיצְךָ וְנַקְדִּישְׁךָ כְּסוֹד שִׂיחַ שַׂרְפֵי קֹדֶש הַמַּקְדִּישִׁים שִׁמְךָ בַּקֹּדֶש

Write in the missing letters for these words that are built from the root קדש.

8. קָ__וֹש

9. __ְדֻשָׁה

10. מְקַדֵּ__

11. נְ__דֵּש

12. בִּקְדֻ__תוֹ

13. __ק__ש

56

קָדוֹשׁ

הַלְלוּיָהּ

יוֹם

Words

name = שֵׁם

all = כָּל

God = אֵל

Word Parts

and = וְ

your = ךָ

in = בְּ

the = הַ

עֲצֹר!

Your teacher will help you with your translation.

אַתָּה קָדוֹשׁ וְשִׁמְךָ קָדוֹשׁ
וּקְדוֹשִׁים בְּכָל־יוֹם יְהַלְלוּךָ סֶּלָה.
בָּרוּךְ אַתָּה יי הָאֵל הַקָּדוֹשׁ.

My best guess at the meaning of this prayer is:

_____

_____

_____

_____

To Talk About

Holy is a hard word to explain.

In the midrash we are told that when God tells us in the Torah You shall be קְדוֹשִׁים (*Lev.* 19.2), it really means You shall be separate or different (*Sifre on Lev.* 19).

Rashi, a medieval commentator, explains that being separate means separating one's self from one's animal urges. God is saying I have planted a spark of my קְדוּשָׁה in you, and that gives you the power to resist the יֵצֶר הָרָע (the temptation to do wrong).

In the midrash we are told, God says, 'When you honor me with your sense of justice, My קְדוּשָׁה lives with you. If you guard two things, justice and ethical actions, I will redeem you with a complete redemption' (*Deut. R.* 5.7).

Questions

1. How can being "separate" or "different" help you come closer to God?
2. How can a "spark of קְדוּשָׁה" keep you from doing wrong?
3. What does "redemption" mean?
4. How can holiness redeem the world?

Go back to page 54-55 and practice the קְדוּשָׁה before you work on this page.

Jacob Visits The Place

מָקוֹם is the Hebrew word for place. הַמָּקוֹם, The Place, is also a name for God.

Jacob left home, came to a place, and made camp. Using a rock for a pillow, he went to sleep and dreamed. In this מָקוֹם he met הַמָּקוֹם. The midrash teaches, Why is God called 'The Place'? Because in every place where there are righteous people God is there. Jacob learned that every מָקוֹם can be a place to discover הַמָּקוֹם.

In his dream Jacob saw a ladder. Its feet were on the ground. Its head was in heaven. Angels were going up and down on the ladder. At the very top of the ladder Jacob saw The Gates of Compassion just below God's throne. When he awoke Jacob said, This place is the Gate of Heaven. This is the place where the gates of heaven open to hear prayers. Here will be בֵּית אֵל, the House of God. Then Jacob said, God is made holy through righteousness.

The angels answered and sang בָּרוּךְ אַתָּה יי הָאֵל הַקָּדוֹשׁ. This was the first time the words that end the קְדוּשָׁה were used (*Gen.* 28.10-22; *P.R.E.* 35).

Questions
1. Why is הַמָּקוֹם (The Place) a name for God?
2. If God is holy to start with, how can our "righteous actions" make God holy?
3. How can knowing this story help you to know where to point your heart when you say the קְדוּשָׁה?

58

1. תִּתְגַּדַּל וְתִתְקַדַּשׁ בְּתוֹךְ יְרוּשָׁלַיִם עִירְךָ

2. כְּשֵׁם שֶׁמַּקְדִּישִׁים אוֹתוֹ בִּשְׁמֵי מָרוֹם

3. כַּכָּתוּב עַל יַד נְבִיאֶךָ וְקָרָא זֶה אֶל זֶה וְאָמַר

4. אַתָּה קָדוֹשׁ וְשִׁמְךָ קָדוֹשׁ וּקְדוֹשִׁים בְּכָל-יוֹם יְהַלְלוּךָ סֶּלָה.

5. קָדוֹשׁ קָדוֹשׁ קָדוֹשׁ יי צְבָאוֹת

6. בָּרוּךְ כְּבוֹד יי מִמְּקוֹמוֹ

7. יִמְלֹךְ יי לְעוֹלָם אֱלֹהַיִךְ צִיּוֹן

8. לְדוֹר וָדוֹר נַגִּיד גָּדְלֶךָ וּלְנֵצַח נְצָחִים

9. מַלְכוּתְךָ כַּדָּבָר הָאָמוּר בְּשִׁירֵי עֻזֶּךָ

10. אָז בְּקוֹל רַעַשׁ גָּדוֹל אַדִּיר וְחָזָק מַשְׁמִיעִים קוֹל

11. מִמְּקוֹמְךָ מַלְכֵּנוּ תוֹפִיעַ וְתִמְלוֹךְ עָלֵינוּ

12. בָּרוּךְ אַתָּה יי הָאֵל הַקָּדוֹשׁ

Some Things to Know About Angels

Two different Hebrew words are used for angel in the Bible. One is מַלְאָךְ, which means messenger. מַלְאָכִים (messengers) can be either heavenly creatures or humans doing holy work. The other word is אֱלֹהִים. It usually means gods but can also means God (referring to The One God.) Most often the phrase בְּנֵי אֵלִים (Children of God) is the way אֱלֹהִים is used for angels.

When you look in the Bible you get two possibilities. Either angels are some kind of heavenly creature or they are people doing God's work.

In the Bible there are other heavenly creatures. Seraphim and cherubim are definitely not people and do have wings.

In the Jewish tradition, angels are not dead people. Traditionally, when Jews die they go back to the Garden of Eden (and not up into heaven) and wait for עוֹלָם הַבָּא (The World to Come).

We learn in the Talmud that most angels exist only to do one job and then they disappear. Some angels those with names are מַלְאֲכֵי הַשָּׁרֵת (ministering angels) who continue to exist to do specific jobs. Mikha'el, Gavri'el, Uri'el, and Rafa'el, as well as the angel of death, are such angels.

The Zohar teaches that angels are a portion of God's strength. It is as if God rips off a small piece of God and sends it off to do a specific job.

The midrash, the Talmud, and the literature that follows in the tradition are filled with stories about angels and stories that use angels. One big angel job is to carry people's prayers up to heaven. Another is to sing and provide human history with a soundtrack.

Maimonides wrote that angels are just a metaphor for God's influence in the world. He did not believe in praying to angels or that they actually exist in a physical form (*Guide*, 2.6, 1.49).

עֲצֹר!

What do you believe about angels?

Go back to page 54-55 and practice the קְדוּשָׁה before you work on this page.

Can you see the three letters כבד in these words?

כָּבוֹד כָּבֵד כָּבֵד

Hebrew builds words out of three-letter roots.

honor = כָּבוֹד

heavy = כָּבֵד

liver = כָּבֵד

Practice these phrases and circle all the words that contain the root כבד.

כַּבֵּד אֶת־אָבִיךָ וְאֶת־אִמֶּךָ   1. בָּרוּךְ שֵׁם כְּבוֹד מַלְכוּתוֹ לְעוֹלָם וָעֶד

מְלֹא כָל־הָאָרֶץ כְּבוֹדוֹ   2. קָדוֹשׁ קָדוֹשׁ קָדוֹשׁ יי צְבָאוֹת

וְחָק עַל מֵצַח כְּבוֹד שֵׁם קָדְשׁוֹ   3. יְהִי כְבוֹד יי לְעוֹלָם יִשְׂמַח יי בְּמַעֲשָׂיו

4. שְׂאוּ שְׁעָרִים רָאשֵׁיכֶם, וּשְׂאוּ פִּתְחֵי עוֹלָם וְיָבוֹא מֶלֶךְ הַכָּבוֹד

5. כְּבוֹד אָב וָאֵם וּגְמִילוּת חֲסָדִים וְהַשְׁכָּמַת בֵּית הַמִּדְרָשׁ שַׁחֲרִית וְעַרְבִית

6. מִתְנַשְּׂאִים לְעֻמַּת שְׂרָפִים, לְעֻמָּתָם בָּרוּךְ יֹאמֵרוּ: בָּרוּךְ כְּבוֹד יי מִמְּקוֹמוֹ

7. יי אָהַבְתִּי מְעוֹן בֵּיתֶךָ וּמְקוֹם מִשְׁכַּן כְּבוֹדֶךָ וַאֲנִי אֶשְׁתַּחֲוֶה וְאֶכְרָעָה

Write in the missing letters for these words that are built from the root כבד.

8. כְּ__וֹדוֹ   9. כַּבֵּ__   10. הַ__ָבוֹד

11. __ְבוֹדֶךָ   12. כָּ__וֹד   13. כְּבוֹ__

61

קָדוֹשׁ קָדוֹשׁ קָדוֹשׁ יי צְבָאוֹת
מְלֹא כָל-הָאָרֶץ כְּבוֹדוֹ.

My best guess at the meaning of this prayer is:

_____

_____

_____

קָדוֹשׁ

אֶרֶץ

כָּבוֹד

Words

Adonai = יי

Hosts = צְבָאוֹת

fill = מְלֹא

all = כָּל

Word Parts

His = ■וֹ

How to Dance the קְדוּשָׁה

When the קְדוּשָׁה is said silently it is just part of the עֲמִידָה. When the קְדוּשָׁה is said out loud with the community it comes with three rules.

(a) It must be started with an invitation. This means that the service leader invites the group to say the prayer, just like the בָּרְכוּ. We do this because when the prophet Isaiah tells of seeing angels, they were calling one to the other (6.3).

(b) It must be said with a *minyan* (a community of at least ten). This is also like the בָּרְכוּ. We do this because of a teaching in Leviticus where God says, "Make me קָדוֹשׁ in a community of Israel" (22.32).

(c) We must stand because Ehud, a judge, stood when he delivered a message from God (*Judges* 3.20). We stand with our feet together because angels stand as if they have one leg (*Ezekiel* 1.7). And we bounce three times when we say "קָדוֹשׁ קָדוֹשׁ קָדוֹשׁ."
We bounce to be like the angels who fluttered around (*Isaiah* 61), to show the lifting of the spirit (*OH* 104.7), and to show that after we do all we can, we are carried by God (*Rav Kook*).

We make ourselves like angels when we say this prayer. Why?

Calling One to the Other: Isaiah's Story

Isaiah was a prophet. He told the following story.

I was in the Temple and looked and I saw God sitting on a throne. Seraphim (angels) were all around serving God. Each one had six wings. Two wings covered their face. Two covered their legs. Two were used to fly. They called to each other:

קָדוֹשׁ קָדוֹשׁ קָדוֹשׁ יי צְבָאוֹת מְלֹא כָל-הָאָרֶץ כְּבוֹדוֹ.

The Temple filled with smoke and I thought I was doomed. I said to myself, "I am not worthy. My lips are unclean."

One seraph flew over to me with a hot coal, touched it to my lips and said, "Your sin is now cleared away." Then I heard God speak and say, "Who shall I send to do my work?" I answered, "Send me." This is when I became a prophet (*Isaiah* 6.1-9).

Questions

1. What did Isaiah learn about God and about angels?
2. The angels' prayer says that "the whole earth is filled with God's honor." What does that mean?
3. What can we learn from this story that helps us say the קְדוּשָׁה?

63

Go back to page 54-55 and practice the קְדוּשָׁה before you work on this page.

Words
Adonai = יי
place = מָקוֹם

Word Parts
from = מִ
His = וֹ■

כָּבוֹד

בָּרוּךְ

בָּרוּךְ כְּבוֹד יי מִמְּקוֹמוֹ.

Your teacher will help you with your translation.

My best guess at the meaning of this part of the prayer is:

_____

_____

_____

Write in the missing word in each of these phrases from the קְדוּשָׁה.

קָדוֹשׁ/בָּרוּךְ	אַתָּה קָדוֹשׁ וְשִׁמְךָ _____	.1
אַהֲבָה/וְתִתְקַדַּשׁ	_____ תִּתְגַּדַּל בְּתוֹךְ יְרוּשָׁלַיִם	.2
לוּלָב/כְּבוֹדוֹ	_____ יי צְבָאוֹת מְלֹא כָל-הָאָרֶץ	.3
בָּרוּךְ/בַּיִת	_____ כְּבוֹד יי מִמְּקוֹמוֹ.	.4
יִמְלֹךְ/נֵר	_____ יי לְעוֹלָם אֱלֹהַיִךְ צִיּוֹן	.5
מְזוּזָה/וּקְדוֹשִׁים	_____ אַתָּה קָדוֹשׁ וְשִׁמְךָ קָדוֹשׁ	.6

64

Taken by the Spirit

Ezekiel was a prophet. He told the following story.

I was in exile in Babylon when the heavens opened and I saw God. There was a storm—a huge cloud flashed fire. In the center of it I saw creatures with four faces, four wings, and a single rigid leg.

God said to me, "Human, take all My words into your heart and listen to them with your ears. Go to the Families-of-Israel who are now in exile and say to them, 'The Eternal, my Master, is speaking to you'—even if they do not listen."

Then a great wind carried me away. I heard behind me the noise of wings beating, and a great roaring voice was singing:

בָּרוּךְ כְּבוֹד יי מִמְּקוֹמוֹ.

A spirit seized me, and I was carried away. This is how I became a prophet (*Ezekiel* 1).

Questions

1. Isaiah saw God in the Temple. Where was Ezekiel when he saw God? Is there a lesson to be learned here?
2. The angels that Ezekiel saw were singing "Blessed be God's honor from God's place." What are they saying about what people have to do to reach God?
3. God told Moses that people cannot see God and live, but both of these prophets tell us that they saw God. What do you think they actually saw?
4. What can we learn from this story that helps us say the קְדוּשָׁה?

Ezekiel Moments/Isaiah Moments

Concept 1: Immanence

Immanence is a fancy way of saying that God is close and that people can feel close to God. Isaiah had an experience of getting close to God. He heard the angels singing מְלֹא כָל־הָאָרֶץ כְּבוֹדוֹ, which teaches that God can be found everywhere. When you feel God in your heart, this is immanence.

Concept 2: Transcendence

Transcendence is a fancy way of saying that God is far away and beyond what a person can understand. Ezekiel's experience of God was one of terror and not quite understanding. He knew that he did not get the whole picture. He heard the angels sing בָּרוּךְ כְּבוֹד יי מִמְּקוֹמוֹ. That suggests that God has a hiding place and only sends out messages. When you feel that God is a big mystery beyond what you can fully get this is transcendence.

Judaism believes that sometimes we feel that God is immanent and sometimes we feel that God is transcendent.

When have you had an Isaiah experience of God knowing that God is close, everywhere, and loving?

_____

_____

_____

_____

_____

When have you had an Ezekiel experience of God knowing that God is hidden, far away, and awesome?

_____

_____

_____

_____

עֲצוֹר!

Go back to page 54-55 and practice the קְדוּשָׁה before you work on this page.

Parts קְדוּשָׁה

1. נְקַדֵּשׁ אֶת־שִׁמְךָ בָּעוֹלָם כְּשֵׁם שֶׁמַּקְדִּישִׁים אוֹתוֹ בִּשְׁמֵי מָרוֹם

2. כַּכָּתוּב עַל יַד נְבִיאֶךָ וְקָרָא זֶה אֶל זֶה וְאָמַר:

3. קָדוֹשׁ קָדוֹשׁ קָדוֹשׁ יי צְבָאוֹת מְלֹא כָל־הָאָרֶץ כְּבוֹדוֹ.

4. אָז בְּקוֹל רַעַשׁ גָּדוֹל אַדִּיר וְחָזָק מַשְׁמִיעִים קוֹל

5. מִתְנַשְּׂאִים לְעֻמַּת שְׂרָפִים לְעֻמָּתָם בָּרוּךְ יֹאמֵרוּ:

6. בָּרוּךְ כְּבוֹד יי מִמְּקוֹמוֹ.

7. יִמְלֹךְ יי לְעוֹלָם אֱלֹהַיִךְ צִיּוֹן לְדֹר וָדֹר, הַלְלוּיָהּ.

8. כִּי אֵל מֶלֶךְ גָּדוֹל וְקָדוֹשׁ אָתָּה. בָּרוּךְ אַתָּה יי הָאֵל הַקָּדוֹשׁ.

Circle the words that mean "holy."

Underline the words that mean "heavy."

Draw a box around the words that mean "bless."

Double underline the words that mean "ruler."

מֶלֶךְ

עוֹלָם

יִמְלֹךְ יי לְעוֹלָם אֱלֹהַיִךְ צִיּוֹן לְדֹר וָדֹר הַלְלוּיָהּ.

Your teacher
will help you
with your
translation.

הַלְלוּיָהּ

My best guess at the meaning of this prayer is:

_____

_____

_____

Words

Adonai = יי

God = אֱלֹהִים

Zion = צִיּוֹן

generation = דֹר

Word Parts

to = לְ

your = ךְ

and = וְ

To Talk About

Philo, a famous Jewish philosopher who lived in Egypt around 50 B.C.E., taught:

When God finished creating the world, God asked the angels if anything was lacking. The angels answered, Everything is perfect except that one thing is missing words that praise God. God agreed with the angels, so God created people.

How can people's praise give something to God that the angels' praise cannot?

Rabbi Ze'ev Einhorn taught in his commentary on the siddur, When Israel says that God is קָדוֹשׁ, it helps to make them קָדוֹשׁ. One purpose of the קְדוּשָׁה is to make us holy.

How does this work? How can saying that God is holy make us holy?

68

Studying a Psalm

Here is a psalm. A psalm is a combination of song, prayer and poem. This one was probably written by King David. He said:

Hallelujah! My soul should thank God...

It is not good to trust in princes or in any people because they cannot save you.

People die. Their breath stops.
   They return to the earth.
   Their thoughts end.

Happy are people who ask God to help...

God made heaven and earth and
   everything there is.

God always stands guard.

God brings justice to the oppressed.

God gives bread to the hungry.

God frees prisoners.

God opens the eyes of the blind.

God straightens those who are bent over.

God loves righteous people...

יִמְלֹךְ יי לְעוֹלָם אֱלֹהַיִךְ צִיּוֹן
לְדֹר וָדֹר הַלְלוּיָהּ.

Psalm 148

Questions

1. What does this psalm give as the central reason for thanking God?
2. The Isaiah and Ezekiel parts of the קְדוּשָׁה talk about seeing God in a vision. According to this psalm, where do we get to learn about God?
3. This psalm ends by calling God אֱלֹהַיִךְ צִיּוֹן—the God of Jerusalem*. What is the connection between a God who helps people and the God of Jerusalem?
4. How can knowing this psalm help you to point your heart when you say the קְדוּשָׁה?

---

*The צִיּוֹן Connection

There are at least three different ways of understanding of אֱלֹהַיִךְ צִיּוֹן. (a) The Messiah will come in Jerusalem it is the beginning of the establishing of God's empire on earth (*Midrash Tehillim ad loc*). (b) One understanding of יְרוּשָׁלַיִם is עִיר שָׁלוֹם (the city that trembles before peace or wholeness). This is the actualization of the best of human values. *Zohar*). (c) צִיּוֹן can also mean the nation of Israel (*Pesikta deRab Kahana*). This has the Psalm end with the God of Israel rather than the God of צִיּוֹן (Jerusalem).

Write Your Own Psalm

Act like King David and write your own psalm. It can be a song or a poem, but it should talk about some special ways of knowing God. It should praise God.

_____

_____

_____

_____

_____

_____

_____

Reviewing the קְדוּשָׁה

Some things to know about the קְדוּשָׁה

It is the third praise בְּרָכָה that begins the עֲמִידָה.

It is known as the angels' prayer and is connected to Jacob's dream.

It is built out of three pieces of the Bible pieces of Isaiah, Ezekiel, and a psalm.

The prayer is said out loud and is acted out between the service leader and the congregation.

Language Learning

We looked at these roots and worked with these words:

Roots: קָדֵשׁ כָּבֵד   Words: הַלְלוּיָה   אֶרֶץ

These are the parts of the קְדוּשָׁה sung by the congregation:

קָדוֹשׁ קָדוֹשׁ קָדוֹשׁ יי צְבָאוֹת מְלֹא כָל־הָאָרֶץ כְּבוֹדוֹ

בָּרוּךְ כְּבוֹד יי מִמְּקוֹמוֹ

יִמְלֹךְ יי לְעוֹלָם אֱלֹהַיִךְ צִיּוֹן לְדֹר וָדֹר, הַלְלוּיָה

עֲצֹר!

70

קְדוּשַׁת הַיּוֹם

The Middle בְּרָכוֹת

The עֲמִידָה is like a sandwich. On the outside are sets of three בְּרָכוֹת, three praise בְּרָכוֹת at the beginning and three thanksgiving בְּרָכוֹת at the end. During the week there are thirteen petition בְּרָכוֹת in the middle. Petition means asking. During the week we ask God for the things that we need. On Shabbat we don't do business with God. We remove these middle בְּרָכוֹת and replace them with a Shabbat prayer.

Shabbat

On Shabbat we say a בְּרָכָה called קְדוּשַׁת הַיּוֹם, the Holiness of the Day. This is very much like the קִדּוּשׁ. It celebrates Shabbat as an opportunity to experience God's holiness and create a sense of holiness of our own.

וְשָׁמְרוּ

The Shabbat commandment was read in the middle of this prayer. But in a period of time when *some* people began to believe that the Ten Commandments were the only important part of the Torah, the Rabbis made a switch. In the evening service they used the וַיְכֻלּוּ, a piece of Torah that comes from the Shabbat part of the story of creation (*Gen.* 2.1-3). On Saturday morning they used the וְשָׁמְרוּ (*Ex.* 31.16-17), which is a lesson about Shabbat that Moses taught soon after the Golden Calf.

Exodus from Egypt. וַיְכֻלּוּ, which is also said as part of the Friday night קִדּוּשׁ, reminds us of the creation connection. וְשָׁמְרוּ, which is part of the Exodus story, is used to introduce the Saturday lunch קִדּוּשׁ. We also sing וְשָׁמְרוּ on Friday night.

In this unit you will learn:
• about the וְשָׁמְרוּ
• נ פ שׁ שׁ ב ת
• two stories

קְדֻשַּׁת הַיּוֹם

Here are two portions of קְדֻשַּׁת הַיּוֹם.

וְשָׁמְרוּ

The Families-of-Israel shall KEEP SHABBAT	וְשָׁמְרוּ בְנֵי יִשְׂרָאֵל אֶת־הַשַּׁבָּת 1.
to MAKE SHABBAT	לַעֲשׂוֹת אֶת־הַשַּׁבָּת 2.
in every generation as a forever COVENANT.	לְדֹרֹתָם בְּרִית עוֹלָם. 3.
Between Me and the Families-of-Israel	בֵּינִי וּבֵין בְּנֵי יִשְׂרָאֵל 4.
SHABBAT is a forever sign.	אוֹת הִיא לְעֹלָם. 5.
Because in six days ADONAI MADE	כִּי שֵׁשֶׁת יָמִים עָשָׂה יי 6.
heavens and earth,	אֶת־הַשָּׁמַיִם וְאֶת־הָאָרֶץ. 7.
but on The Seventh Day	וּבַיּוֹם הַשְּׁבִיעִי 8.
God had a SHABBAT and re-SOULED.	שָׁבַת וַיִּנָּפַשׁ. 9.

אֱלֹהֵינוּ וֵאלֹהֵי אֲבוֹתֵינוּ

Our God and God of our Ancestors	אֱלֹהֵינוּ וֵאלֹהֵי אֲבוֹתֵינוּ 10.
enjoy our REST.	רְצֵה בִמְנוּחָתֵנוּ. 11.
Make us Holy through Your MITZVOT	קַדְּשֵׁנוּ בְּמִצְוֹתֶיךָ 12.
and give us a piece of Your TORAH.	וְתֵן חֶלְקֵנוּ בְּתוֹרָתֶךָ 13.
NOURISH us with Your goodness	שַׂבְּעֵנוּ מִטּוּבֶךָ 14.
And MAKE-US-HAPPY through Your REDEMPTION	וְשַׂמְּחֵנוּ בִּישׁוּעָתֶךָ 15.
PURIFY our hearts to Your WORK in truth.	וְטַהֵר לִבֵּנוּ לְעָבְדְּךָ בֶּאֱמֶת. 16.
ADONAI our God, give-us-as-an-INHERITANCE	וְהַנְחִילֵנוּ יי אֱלֹהֵינוּ 17.
in LOVE and because You WANT it—Your HOLY SHABBAT.	בְּאַהֲבָה וּבְרָצוֹן שַׁבַּת קָדְשֶׁךָ 18.
May Israel REST on it MAKING Your NAME holy.	וְיָנוּחוּ בָה יִשְׂרָאֵל מְקַדְּשֵׁי שְׁמֶךָ. 19.
Blessed be You ADONAI the One-Who-makes SHABBAT HOLY.	בָּרוּךְ אַתָּה יי מְקַדֵּשׁ הַשַּׁבָּת. 20.

This is the Saturday morning version of this prayer.

Shabbat in Egypt

Moses came and told Pharaoh to Let my people go.   Pharaoh laughed and said No. To make matters worse, Pharaoh then told the Families-of-Israel that they had to work harder. Before they had to make mud bricks using straw that other people had cut and brought to the river's edge. Now the Jews had to make the same number of bricks every day, but they had to cut and haul their own straw. The Families-of-Israel got really mad at Moses because he had not set them free. Instead, he made things worse.

Moses went back to Pharaoh and asked, How would you like to get twice as much work out of your slaves? Pharaoh nodded. Moses said, You have a choice. Kill more and more of your slaves by working them to death or give them one day a week off to recover. Then you can work them twice as hard. Pharaoh asked, What day should it be? Moses smiled and said, Start on Friday night. From that day on, Israel had Shabbat in Egypt. It was their first taste of freedom (*Exodus Rabbah* 1.28).

Questions

1. What is the connection between Shabbat and Egypt?
2. How can knowing this story help you point your heart when you say both the קִדּוּשׁ and the קְדוּשַׁת הַיּוֹם (with וְשָׁמְרוּ) on Shabbat?

73

שׁוֹמֵר

בָּנִים

יִשְׂרָאֵל

שַׁבָּת

עָשָׂה

עוֹלָם

עֲצֹר!

Your teacher will help you with your translation.

וְשָׁמְרוּ בְנֵי יִשְׂרָאֵל אֶת־הַשַּׁבָּת
לַעֲשׂוֹת אֶת־הַשַּׁבָּת לְדֹרֹתָם בְּרִית עוֹלָם.
בֵּינִי וּבֵין בְּנֵי יִשְׂרָאֵל אוֹת הִיא לְעֹלָם.

My best guess at the meaning of this prayer is:

_____

_____

_____

To Talk About

This Torah text says לַעֲשׂוֹת אֶת הַשַּׁבָּת to make Shabbat. In Jewish English we often talk about making Shabbat. That usually means cooking and cleaning, or Shabbat preparation. In the Midrash Rabbi Eliezer ben Perata taught, A person who 'observes' Shabbat is a person who 'makes' Shabbat.

What kinds of things do you have to do to turn Friday night and Saturday into Shabbat? What kinds of things do you have to not do to make them Shabbat?

Word Parts	Words
to = לְ	generation = דֹרֹת
the = הַ	covenant = בְּרִית
and = וְ\וּ	between = בֵּין
me = ■נִי	she (Shabbat) = הִיא

אוֹתִיוֹת

74

Go back to page 72 and read the קְדוּשַׁת הַיּוֹם before you work on this page.

Can you see the three letters שׁבת in these words?

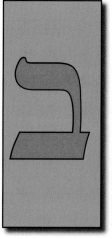 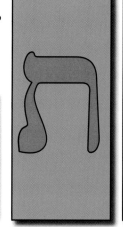

שָׁבַת   יִשְׁבֹּת   שַׁבָּת

Shabbat = שַׁבָּת

cease work = יִשְׁבֹּת

(He) rested = שָׁבַת

Practice these phrases and circle all the words that contain the root שׁבת.

1. וְשָׁמְרוּ בְנֵי־יִשְׂרָאֵל אֶת־הַשַּׁבָּת   כִּי בוֹ שָׁבַת צוּר עוֹלָמִים

2. וַיִּשְׁבֹּת בַּיּוֹם הַשְּׁבִיעִי מִכָּל־מְלַאכְתּוֹ   בָּרוּךְ אַתָּה יְיָ מְקַדֵּשׁ הַשַּׁבָּת

Can you see the three letters נפשׁ in these words?

נֶפֶשׁ   נַפְשְׁךָ   וַיִּנָּפַשׁ

soul = נֶפֶשׁ

your soul = נַפְשְׁךָ

and He rested = וַיִּנָּפַשׁ

Practice these phrases and circle all the words that contain the root נפשׁ.

3. יְדִיד נֶפֶשׁ אָב הָרַחֲמָן   וּבַיּוֹם הַשְּׁבִיעִי שָׁבַת וַיִּנָּפַשׁ

4. בְּכָל־לְבָבְךָ וּבְכָל־נַפְשְׁךָ וּבְכָל־מְאֹדֶךָ   בְּכָל־לְבַבְכֶם וּבְכָל־נַפְשְׁכֶם

6

 שֵׁשׁ

יוֹם

עָשָׂה

אֶרֶץ

7

שֶׁבַע

שַׁבָּת

Your teacher will help you with your translation.

כִּי שֵׁשֶׁת יָמִים עָשָׂה יי
אֶת־הַשָּׁמַיִם וְאֶת־הָאָרֶץ
וּבַיּוֹם הַשְּׁבִיעִי שָׁבַת וַיִּנָּפַשׁ.

My best guess at the meaning of this prayer is:

_____

_____

_____

To Talk About

Rabbi Shimon ben Lakish looked at the word וַיִּנָּפַשׁ. While it sometimes is translated as "refreshed," it comes from the word נֶפֶשׁ, which means "soul." In the Talmud he taught, "On Friday night God gives us a נְשָׁמָה יְתֵרָה an extra portion of soul. On Saturday night, after Shabbat, God takes it back."

Questions

1. What does it feel like to have an extra piece of soul on Shabbat?
2. How does Shabbat help us to experience our spiritual side?
3. How can knowing about the נְשָׁמָה יְתֵרָה help you point your heart when you say the וְשָׁמְרוּ?

נֶפֶשׁ

Word Parts	Words
the = הַ	because = כִּי
and = וְ\וּ	heavens = שָׁמַיִם
in/with = בְּ	

The First Shabbat

In the beginning, God was alone. So God created the angels, the other heavenly creatures, and people, too. The first thing God created was light. It was a special kind of light one that came directly from God. On the fourth day of creation God created the sun, the moon, and the stars. The original light was hidden away.

On the first Shabbat God stopped working and gathered all of creation. The angel of Shabbat got to sit on the throne of glory, and all of the angels got to rest. They gathered round and folded their six wings. On the seventh day they could not sing. God brought Adam and Eve up to heaven to join in the Shabbat celebration. They were the ones who began to sing, It is good to give thanks to God, the words that later started the Shabbat psalm. The angels joined in.

God told Adam and Eve that a piece of the Garden of Eden is in every Shabbat. God said, During Shabbat you will be able to taste the world to come. God then decided that a little bit of the original hidden light would be released into the world every Shabbat.

(Assembled through the notes in Louis Ginzberg's *Legends of the Jews*).

Questions
1. What is the special connection between Shabbat and people?
2. How does Shabbat connect us to God?
3. How can knowing this story help us to point our hearts when we say קְדוּשַׁת הַיּוֹם in the עֲמִידָה on Shabbat?

Reviewing קְדוּשַׁת הַיּוֹם

Some things to know about קְדוּשַׁת הַיּוֹם

On Shabbat this prayer replaces the thirteen middle בְּרָכוֹת in the עֲמִידָה because we don't do business with God on Shabbat.

It celebrates the holiness of Shabbat. Different versions are said at each of the Shabbat services.

At the heart of the עֶרֶב שַׁבָּת version is וַיְכֻלּוּ, a piece of Torah (*Genesis* 2.1-3) that emphasizes the connection between Shabbat and creation.

At the heart of the Shabbat morning version is the וְשָׁמְרוּ, a piece of Torah (*Exodus* 31:16-17) that emphasizes the Shabbat and Exodus connection.

Language Learning

Among the words and word parts we worked with in this unit are:

Roots:

Words:
 שֵׁשׁ
 אוֹתִיּוֹת
  עוֹלָם
 עָשָׂה
 שַׁבָּת
 יִשְׂרָאֵל
 בָּנִים
 שׁוֹמֵר

 נֶפֶשׁ
 שֶׁבַע
 אֶרֶץ
  יוֹם

The Heart of the Prayer

At the heart of the Shabbat morning version is:

וְשָׁמְרוּ בְנֵי יִשְׂרָאֵל אֶת־הַשַּׁבָּת לַעֲשׂוֹת אֶת־הַשַּׁבָּת לְדֹרֹתָם בְּרִית עוֹלָם.
בֵּינִי וּבֵין בְּנֵי יִשְׂרָאֵל אוֹת הִיא לְעֹלָם. כִּי שֵׁשֶׁת יָמִים עָשָׂה יי
אֶת־הַשָּׁמַיִם וְאֶת־הָאָרֶץ, וּבַיּוֹם הַשְּׁבִיעִי שָׁבַת וַיִּנָּפַשׁ.

בִּרְכַּת הוֹדָאָה

The Final Three

The עֲמִידָה ends with three final בְּרָכוֹת that are blessings of "thanksgiving." These final three are said on both Shabbat and weekdays. They are:

בִּרְכַּת עֲבוֹדָה, which thanks God for hearing our prayers and hopes that our worship is acceptable.

בִּרְכַּת הוֹדָאָה (or מוֹדִים), which thanks God for the opportunity to say thank you.

בִּרְכַּת שָׁלוֹם, which thanks God for the possibility of peace (and asks God to help us finally achieve peace).

מוֹדִים

בִּרְכַּת הוֹדָאָה starts with the words "מוֹדִים אֲנַחְנוּ לָךְ." It means "We are thankful to You." These words lead us to the heart of this prayer: that God is the source of our lives and of all that is good in our lives.

בִּרְכַּת הוֹדָאָה was part of the original service in the Temple. At the end of a day of sacrificing the priests would say a few prayers that included the Ten Commandments, the שְׁמַע, the "מוֹדִים," and the priestly blessing for peace. When the Rabbis replaced sacrifices with the prayer service, מוֹדִים was still used as part of the ending.

בִּרְכַּת הוֹדָאָה is:

the eighteenth בְּרָכָה in the עֲמִידָה (the sixth בְּרָכָה on Shabbat).

a בְּרָכָה where it is a custom to bow at its beginning and at its end.

a בְּרָכָה that has a second version that is said by the congregation if the עֲמִידָה is repeated out loud.

a place where a special Hanukkah prayer is added.

an acting out of the story of King Solomon celebrating the grand opening of the Temple in Jerusalem.

It thanks God for four things: our lives; our souls; the miracles in our lives; and the gifts that happen evening, morning and afternoon.

Miracles

Dr. Eli Munk wrote that בִּרְכַּת הוֹדָאָה is a thank you for "the visible and invisible miracles that occur the thousands of gifts that are woven into the texture of our daily lives."

Question: What are visible and invisible miracles?

79

בִּרְכַּת הוֹדָאָה

English	Hebrew	#
We give THANKS to YOU	מוֹדִים אֲנַחְנוּ לָךְ	1.
that YOU are the ONE, ADONAI our God	שָׁאַתָּה הוּא יי אֱלֹהֵינוּ	2.
and the God of our ancestors forever and always.	וֵאלֹהֵי אֲבוֹתֵינוּ לְעוֹלָם וָעֶד	3.
YOU are the rock of our lives, the shield of our future.	צוּר חַיֵּינוּ מָגֵן יִשְׁעֵנוּ	4.
YOU are the ONE from generation to generation.	אַתָּה הוּא לְדוֹר וָדוֹר.	5.
We give THANKS to YOU and tell stories that celebrate YOU,	נוֹדֶה לְךָ וּנְסַפֵּר תְּהִלָּתֶךָ	6.
(a) For our LIVES that are delivered into YOUR hands	עַל חַיֵּינוּ הַמְּסוּרִים בְּיָדֶךָ	7.
(b) For our SOULS that visit YOU	וְעַל נִשְׁמוֹתֵינוּ הַפְּקוּדוֹת לָךְ	8.
(c) For YOUR MIRACLES that are with us every day	וְעַל נִסֶּיךָ שֶׁבְּכָל־יוֹם עִמָּנוּ	9.
and (d) for YOUR WONDERS and YOUR GOOD STUFF	וְעַל נִפְלְאוֹתֶיךָ וְטוֹבוֹתֶיךָ	10.
that are happening all the time, evening, morning and noon.	שֶׁבְּכָל־עֵת עֶרֶב וָבֹקֶר וְצָהֳרָיִם.	11.
The GOOD THING is that don't ever take away YOUR MERCY,	הַטּוֹב כִּי לֹא כָלוּ רַחֲמֶיךָ	12.
and in mercy that YOU don't remove YOUR KINDNESS	וְהַמְרַחֵם כִּי לֹא תַמּוּ חֲסָדֶיךָ	13.
to eternity we are lined up with YOU.	מֵעוֹלָם קִוִּינוּ לָךְ.	14.
For all this	וְעַל כֻּלָּם	15.
May YOUR NAME be blessed and made great, our Ruler	יִתְבָּרַךְ וְיִתְרוֹמַם שִׁמְךָ מַלְכֵּנוּ	16.
constantly forever and always.	תָּמִיד לְעוֹלָם וָעֶד.	17.
And all life praises YOU. Selah.	וְכֹל הַחַיִּים יוֹדוּךָ סֶּלָה	18.
And may YOUR NAME be celebrated with truth.	וִיהַלְלוּ אֶת־שִׁמְךָ בֶּאֱמֶת	19.
You are THE GOD, our SAVIOR, and our HELPER. Selah.	הָאֵל יְשׁוּעָתֵנוּ וְעֶזְרָתֵנוּ סֶלָה.	20.
Blessed are YOU, ADONAI,	בָּרוּךְ אַתָּה יי	20.
the ONE whose NAME is GOOD	הַטּוֹב שִׁמְךָ	21.
and to YOU it is right to SAY THANKS.	וּלְךָ נָאֶה לְהוֹדוֹת.	22.

Words

and more = וָעֶד

to you = לְךָ

Word Parts

that/which = שֶׁ/שָׁ

אָב

הוּא

אַתָּה

אֲנַחְנוּ

מוֹדֶה

מוֹדִים אֲנַחְנוּ לָךְ שָׁאַתָּה הוּא יי אֱלֹהֵינוּ
וֵאלֹהֵי אֲבוֹתֵינוּ לְעוֹלָם וָעֶד.

Your teacher will help you with your translation.

My best guess at the meaning of this prayer is:

_____

_____

_____

The Choreography

The Talmud teaches that we are required to bow at the beginning and the end of בִּרְכַּת הוֹדָאָה as a way of acknowledging God's presence in our lives. We are told that if someone does not bend when he or she says מוֹדִים, his or her spine will turn into a snake.

Rashi explains that this does not mean that a person's spine will grow soft and bend. Rather, it means that he or she will become like the snake in the Adam and Eve story. The snake tried to convince Eve that what God wanted did not make a difference. He told her to do what she wanted to do rather than be grateful for everything that God did. When we don't bow before God and say thank you, we become the snake (*Brakhot* 34a).

Question: What does it mean to become the snake?

David's Memory Makes a Difference

David took the city of Jerusalem and wanted to build God's House there, but God said "No." God was upset about all the blood that David had spilled. God was also upset that he had done a bad thing in stealing Batsheva from her husband. David asked, "Will you ever forgive me?" God answered, "Eventually, but your son, Solomon, will be the one to build the Temple."

When the Temple was finished and ready for its dedication, Solomon tried to bring the Ark of the Covenant into the Holy of Holies. The gates refused to open. Solomon said, "Lift up your heads. Open up the gates. Let in the Ruler with Honor (*Psalms* 24:9-10)". The gates stayed shut and asked him, "Who is the Ruler with Honor?" Solomon said, "The Ten Commandments that are in the ark." The gates said, "Try again." Solomon said, "The Holy One Who often comes close to us when we are near the Ark." The gates didn't move and said, "What is your third guess?" Solomon said, "David, my father, who was God's servant." The gates opened. The Ark went into the Holy of Holies. David was forgiven, and the angels sang, "בָּרוּךְ אַתָּה יי הַטּוֹב שִׁמְךָ וּלְךָ נָאֶה לְהוֹדוֹת, Praised are You Adonai, The Good-One is Your name and it feels good to praise You." (*Shabbat* 30a; *Shebolei Leket* 18)

Questions

1. The end of this story shows that God forgave David. Why did the angels sing "It feels good to praise God"? (Clue: Remember, David wrote the Psalms—Songs of Praise.)
2. How does knowing this story help you point your heart when you say בִּרְכַּת הוֹדָאָה?

Reviewing בִּרְכַּת הוֹדָאָה

Some things to know:

- The last three בְּרָכוֹת in the עֲמִידָה are בְּרָכוֹת of thanksgiving.
- מוֹדִים is the next to last בְּרָכָה in the עֲמִידָה.
- Its theme is "thank you" and it is rooted in King Solomon knowing his father's prayers were accepted.

Words:

 עֲצֹר!

 אָב

 הוּא

 אַתָּה

 אֲנַחְנוּ

מוֹדָה

בְּרְכַּת שָׁלוֹם

בְּרְכַּת שָׁלוֹם is:

- the last of three thanksgiving בְּרְכוֹת that end the עֲמִידָה and the very last בְּרָכָה in the עֲמִידָה.

- a בְּרָכָה that asks for both world peace and personal inner peace.

- a prayer that has two versions.
  In Ashkenazic traditions, שִׂים שָׁלוֹם is said at morning services. שָׁלוֹם רָב is said at afternoon, מוּסָף and evening services. Sefardim do it differently.

At the end of the service in the Temple the כֹּהֲנִים (priests) would bless the people. This was their way of performing a biblical מִצְוָה, "The כֹּהֲנִים should put My Name on the People of Israel–and I will bless them" (*Num.* 6.27). שָׁלוֹם is one of God's names.

This was done as part of a ceremony called *duchinin*. The כֹּהֲנִים would come up on the bimah, cover their heads with their tallitot, spread their fingers making a "שׁ"–and say the words of the priestly benediction. This ceremony is still done weekly in some Orthodox synagogues in Israel and Sefardic synagogues. In some Conservative and Orthodox synagogues elsewhere this is done only on festivals. Many Reform synagogues have dropped the ceremony, but Reform rabbis often still bless the congregation with these words at the end of services. Jewish parents still use this biblical בְּרָכָה to bless their children on Shabbat.

When the Temple was destroyed and the עֲמִידָה replaced the sacrifices, בְּרְכַּת שָׁלוֹם became its final בְּרָכָה. בְּרְכַּת שָׁלוֹם became the day-to-day replacement for בִּרְכַּת-כֹּהֲנִים in the Temple. This pattern followed a lesson taught by Rabbi Eleazar ha-Kappar, "Great is peace. It is the end of all בְּרָכוֹת" (*Sifre, Numbers*, 42).

Why should שָׁלוֹם be "the end" of all בְּרָכוֹת?

FOOTNOTE: Ashkenazic Jews are those who came from Christian countries in Northern and Eastern Europe. Sefardic Jews are those who come from Moslem countries in Spain, Northern Africa, and the Middle East. Some Sefardic Jews moved to Holland, Rome, and Rhodes.

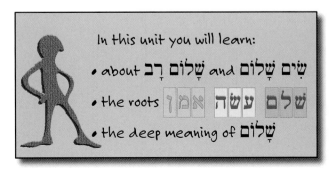

In this unit you will learn:
- about שִׂים שָׁלוֹם and שָׁלוֹם רָב
- the roots שׁלם עשׂה אמן
- the deep meaning of שָׁלוֹם

שִׂים שָׁלוֹם

Put PEACE, GOODNESS & BLESSING	שִׂים שָׁלוֹם (בָּעוֹלָם) טוֹבָה וּבְרָכָה .1
FAVOR, KINDNESS and MERCY	חֵן וָחֶסֶד וְרַחֲמִים .2
on us & on all Israel, Your people.	עָלֵינוּ וְעַל כָּל־יִשְׂרָאֵל עַמֶּךָ. .3
BLESS us, our PARENT, all of us as ONE	בָּרְכֵנוּ אָבִינוּ כֻּלָּנוּ כְּאֶחָד .4
in the light of YOUR FACE	בְּאוֹר פָּנֶיךָ, .5
because in the light of YOUR FACE You gave us	כִּי בְאוֹר פָּנֶיךָ נָתַתָּ לָּנוּ .6
ADONAI, our God	יי אֱלֹהֵינוּ. .7
The TORAH of life, and the LOVE-of-KINDNESS	תּוֹרַת חַיִּים וְאַהֲבַת חֶסֶד, .8
and JUSTICE and BLESSING and MERCY	וּצְדָקָה וּבְרָכָה וְרַחֲמִים .9
and LIFE and PEACE.	וְחַיִּים וְשָׁלוֹם. .10
And (may it be) good in YOUR EYES	וְטוֹב בְּעֵינֶיךָ .11
to bless Your people Israel	לְבָרֵךְ אֶת עַמְּךָ יִשְׂרָאֵל .12
in all times, in all hours, with Your PEACE.	בְּכָל־עֵת וּבְכָל־שָׁעָה בִּשְׁלוֹמֶךָ. .13
Praised be You, ADONAI	בָּרוּךְ אַתָּה יי .14
The ONE-Who-BLESSES God's people Israel with PEACE.	הַמְבָרֵךְ אֶת־עַמּוֹ יִשְׂרָאֵל בַּשָּׁלוֹם. .15

The כֹּהֲנִים would use these words to bless the people:

יְבָרֶכְךָ יי וְיִשְׁמְרֶךָ
May ADONAI bless you and keep you

יָאֵר יי פָּנָיו אֵלֶיךָ וִיחֻנֶּךָּ
May ADONAI'S face shine on you and give you goodness

יִשָּׂא יי פָּנָיו אֵלֶיךָ וְיָשֵׂם לְךָ שָׁלוֹם
May ADONAI'S face turn towards you and give you peace

Some of these words were woven into the שִׂים שָׁלוֹם. Can you find the places where:
the root ברך is used?
the word שָׁלוֹם is used?
the image of God's פָּנִים (face) is used?

The reason that this בְּרָכָה for peace for all Israel was attached to the end of the עֲמִידָה is that at the end of every service in the Temple the כֹּהֲנִים would bless the people of Israel. The עֲמִידָה was introduced by the Rabbis to parallel the Temple service (*Abudraham*).

Why is it good to connect our services to the services that used to be in the Temple?

Can you see the three letters שלם in these words?

מְשַׁלֵּם שְׁלֵמָה שָׁלוֹם

Hebrew builds words out of three-letter roots.

peace = שָׁלוֹם

complete = שְׁלֵמָה

pay = מְשַׁלֵּם

Practice these phrases and circle all the words that contain the root שָׁלֵם.

1. עוֹשֶׂה שָׁלוֹם בִּמְרוֹמָיו   בְּכָל־עֵת וּבְכָל־שָׁעָה בִּשְׁלוֹמֶךָ

2. שָׁלוֹם רָב עַל־יִשְׂרָאֵל עַמְּךָ   בָּרוּךְ מְשַׁלֵּם שָׂכָר טוֹב לִירֵאָיו

3. אָבִינוּ מַלְכֵּנוּ, שְׁלַח רְפוּאָה שְׁלֵמָה לְפָנֶיךָ

4. בְּסֵפֶר חַיִּים בְּרָכָה וְשָׁלוֹם וּפַרְנָסָה טוֹבָה

5. בּוֹאֲכֶם לְשָׁלוֹם מַלְאֲכֵי הַשָּׁלוֹם מַלְאֲכֵי עֶלְיוֹן

6. וּשְׁמֹר צֵאתֵנוּ וּבוֹאֵנוּ לְחַיִּים וּלְשָׁלוֹם מֵעַתָּה וְעַד עוֹלָם.

7. שִׂים שָׁלוֹם טוֹבָה וּבְרָכָה חֵן וָחֶסֶד וְרַחֲמִים עָלֵינוּ וְעַל כָּל־יִשְׂרָאֵל

Write in the missing letters for these words that are built from the root שָׁלֵם.

8. ___ָלוֹם

9. מְשַׁלֵּ___

10. שְׁ___ֵ___מָה

11. שָׁ___מוֹת

12. ___ַלְמְתִּי

13. בִּשְׁלוֹ___ָךְ

85

Making Words from Parts

Here are some words that have been broken into parts.

עָלֵינוּ = עַל + נוּ

עַמְּךָ = עַם + ךָ

Match the words on the right to their basic forms on the left.

בָּרֵךְ	עָלֵינוּ
עַם	פָּנֶיךָ
כֹּל	אָבִינוּ
עֵינַיִם	עַמְּךָ
אֶל	בְּעֵינֶיךָ
פָּנִים	כֻּלָּנוּ
אָב	בַּרְכֵנוּ
שָׁלוֹם	בִּשְׁלוֹמֶךָ
עַל	אֱלֹהֵינוּ

Go back to page 84 and practice the שִׂים שָׁלוֹם before you work on this page.

Your teacher will help you with your translation.

שִׂים שָׁלוֹם טוֹבָה וּבְרָכָה חֵן וָחֶסֶד
וְרַחֲמִים עָלֵינוּ וְעַל כָּל־יִשְׂרָאֵל עַמֶּךָ

My best guess at the meaning of this prayer is:

_____

_____

_____

שָׁלוֹם

טוֹב

בָּרוּךְ

חֶסֶד

עַל

Words

put = שִׂים
favor = חֵן
mercy = רַחֲמִים
nation = עַם

Word Parts

and = וְ/וָ
your = ךָ
us = נוּ

To Talk About

There is a tradition that the Kohanim asked six blessings of God for the people Israel. This is because there are six verbs in בִּרְכַּת כֹּהֲנִים. Each verb is a request. This prayer begins by asking God for six things:

שָׁלוֹם   טוֹבָה
בְּרָכָה   חֵן
חֶסֶד   רַחֲמִים

Create your own explanation for each of these. How is each different? Why is it important to have each on the list?

Quiet vs. Wholeness

The word שָׁלוֹם comes from the Hebrew root שלם, which means "whole" or complete".

Here are some of the words that come from שלם.

שָׁלוֹם = peace   שְׁלֵמוּת = wholeness

שָׁלוֹם = hello   תַשְׁלוּם = payment

שָׁלוֹם = goodbye   מֻשְׁלָם = perfect

שְׁלֹמֹה = Solomon   נִשְׁלַם = was completed

The English word "peace" comes from the Latin word "*Pax*," which means "quiet."

Questions

1. Based on these different examples, what does the root [שלם] mean?
2. How is "goodbye" connected to "perfect"?
3. What is the difference between the Hebrew idea of "שָׁלוֹם" and the English idea of "peace"?

Praying for Shalom

When one prays for שָׁלוֹם, one should pray that there be no fighting, no jealousy, hatred or rivalry, but that all should love one another and be completely united in love, unity, and friendship. All should be of one spirit and committed to the מִצְוָה, "You shall love your neighbor as yourself." (*Leviticus* 19.18)

One should pray to be entirely free of anger and to be able to humble toward all, because where there is anger there is no peace. (*Ya'arot Devash*)

Questions

1. This commentary suggests that when one says בִּרְכַּת שָׁלוֹם, one should pray for two different things. What are they?
2. What is the connection between "internal completeness" and "world peace"?

88

Entering the Land of Israel

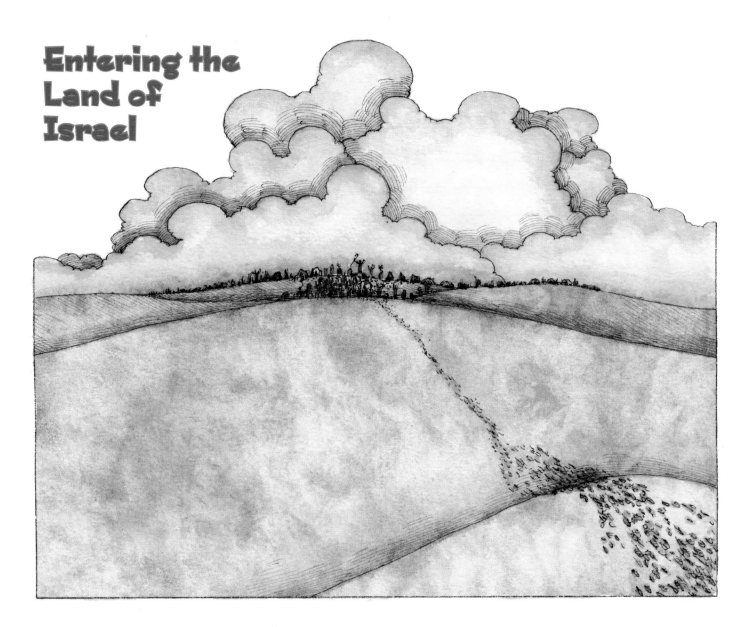

It is not a long walk from Egypt to Israel, yet it took the Families-of-Israel forty years. It took a long time because it took the Families-of-Israel a long time to become a holy nation.

God could have led them along the Mediterranean. That is the quick way, but God chose a longer road. God said, "If I lead them directly into the Land of Israel, they will become selfish. These former slaves will only think about what they have and what they can have. They will worry about their own fields and their own vineyards, and they will forget to take care of each other. They will forget about the Torah. If they camp together in the wilderness--if they have to ration water and gather their own food every day they will gain discipline and become a community."

Just about as soon as they crossed the Reed Sea the people complained about the lack of water. They were afraid that they would not have enough. God talked to them directly at Mount Sinai, and within two months they were making a Golden Calf. They were worried that no one was leading them. The rebellions kept coming. Even though there was more than enough miracle food, manna, the people complained about the lack of meat. Another time they complained about the lack of "garlic, onions, and fish that they used to eat for free in Egypt."

When God asked the families to spy out the Land of Israel, the people panicked. They chickened out. They stopped trusting God. No faith. They said, We can't do it. God extended the training program. The Families-of-Israel spent forty years in Sinai. They gathered manna every day except Shabbat. They stood in line to get water. They studied Torah with Moses and used it to solve the problems that came with living together.

Finally, after all that waiting, God told them it was time to enter the Land. For forty years they had owned nothing. They had been homeless wanderers. They had rebelled and rebelled. When Joshua led Israel into the Land they spent seven years fighting. At the end of seven years they were sick of war. They had had enough. At that moment he angels looked into Israel's hearts. The angels saw that Israel had grown. They had learned to live together and trust God. They had come to understand that שָׁלוֹם was the most important thing. At that moment the angels sang for the first time, בָּרוּךְ אַתָּה יי עֹשֶׂה הַשָּׁלוֹם (Shebbolei Leket, chapter 18 and other midrashim).

Questions
1. How did the years in the desert help the Families-of-Israel build up a sense of שָׁלוֹם?
2. When have you been like the Families-of-Israel, taking a long time to be ready to enter a "Promised Land"?
3. How can knowing this story help you point your heart when you say בִּרְכַּת שָׁלוֹם?

90

שָׁלוֹם רָב

Much PEACE	שָׁלוֹם רָב 1.
on Israel, Your People, put forever	עַל יִשְׂרָאֵל עַמְּךָ תָּשִׂים לְעוֹלָם. 2.
Because You are the ONE, the RULER	כִּי אַתָּה הוּא מֶלֶךְ 3.
The Master of all PEACE.	אָדוֹן לְכָל־הַשָּׁלוֹם. 4.
And (may it be) good in YOUR EYES	וְטוֹב בְּעֵינֶיךָ 5.
to bless Your people Israel	לְבָרֵךְ אֶת עַמְּךָ יִשְׂרָאֵל 6.
in all times, in all hours, with Your PEACE.	בְּכָל־עֵת וּבְכָל־שָׁעָה בִּשְׁלוֹמֶךָ. 7.
Praised be You, ADONAI	בָּרוּךְ אַתָּה יי 8.
The ONE-Who-BLESSES God's people Israel with PEACE.	הַמְבָרֵךְ אֶת־עַמּוֹ יִשְׂרָאֵל בַּשָּׁלוֹם. 9.

The first line of שָׁלוֹם רָב versus the first line of שִׂים שָׁלוֹם

Match the words that are more or less the same in each of these prayers.

שָׁלוֹם רָב	שִׂים שָׁלוֹם טוֹבָה וּבְרָכָה
עַל יִשְׂרָאֵל עַמְּךָ	חֵן וָחֶסֶד וְרַחֲמִים
תָּשִׂים לְעוֹלָם.	עָלֵינוּ וְעַל כָּל־יִשְׂרָאֵל עַמֶּךָ

word parts

to/for = לְ

the = הַ

words

He = הוּא

master = אָדוֹן

all = כָּל

much = רָב

nation = עַם

put = שִׂים

because = כִּי

Your teacher will help you with your translation.

שָׁלוֹם רָב עַל יִשְׂרָאֵל עַמְּךָ תָּשִׂים לְעוֹלָם
כִּי אַתָּה הוּא מֶלֶךְ אָדוֹן לְכָל־הַשָּׁלוֹם.

My best guess at the meaning of this prayer is:

_____

_____

_____

מֶלֶךְ   אַתָּה   עוֹלָם   יִשְׂרָאֵל   עַל   שָׁלוֹם

Practice these phrases from עֹשֶׂה שָׁלוֹם and שָׁלוֹם רָב ,שִׂים שָׁלוֹם.

7. עֹשֶׂה שָׁלוֹם בִּמְרוֹמָיו	1. בָּרוּךְ אַתָּה יי עֹשֶׂה הַשָּׁלוֹם
8. הוּא יַעֲשֶׂה שָׁלוֹם עָלֵינוּ	2. טוֹבָה וּבְרָכָה חֵן וָחֶסֶד וְרַחֲמִים
9. וְעַל כָּל־יִשְׂרָאֵל, וְאִמְרוּ אָמֵן	3. בָּרְכֵנוּ אָבִינוּ כֻּלָּנוּ כְּאֶחָד
10. כִּי בְאוֹר פָּנֶיךָ נָתַתָּ לָנוּ יי אֱלֹהֵינוּ	4. בְּכָל־עֵת וּבְכָל־שָׁעָה בִּשְׁלוֹמֶךָ
11. עַל יִשְׂרָאֵל עַמְּךָ תָּשִׂים לְעוֹלָם	5. וְטוֹב בְּעֵינֶיךָ לְבָרֵךְ אֶת־עַמְּךָ
12. וּבְרָכָה וְרַחֲמִים וְחַיִּים וְשָׁלוֹם	6. תּוֹרַת חַיִּים וְאַהֲבַת חֶסֶד וּצְדָקָה

Jacob and Esau Make Peace

From before their birth, brothers Jacob and Esau struggled with each other. As unborn babies they wrestled in the womb. Jacob first tricked Esau out of his birthright and then later stole his father's blessing. Jacob ran away from home and went back to *Padam Ari-um* in the old country to keep his brother from killing him. He spent twenty years away from home, married two women and had twelve children. Before he headed back home he prayed to God, Let me return to my father's home in peace (*Gen.* 28.21).

When Jacob and his holy family were about to meet Esau and his army of four hundred was moving toward him Jacob prepared three things: peace-offerings, a prayer, and to fight back. He spent the night alone and wound up wrestling with a stranger who for him was the spirit of his brother. He walked away crippled and with a new name, יִשְׂרָאֵל. When Esau came ready for war he saw a crippled man surrounded by women and children. He felt safe. He was transformed, too. Both brothers were now ready to make peace. At that moment the angels sang, שָׁלוֹם רַב עַל יִשְׂרָאֵל תָּשִׂים לְעוֹלָם (*Tanḥuma, Yashan* 6; *Kallah Rabbati* 3; *Rashbam ad loc*).

Questions

1. What made Jacob ready to make peace? What made Esau ready to make peace?
2. Explain the connection between inner peace and political peace in this story.
3. How can knowing this story help you know where to point your heart when you say בִּרְכַּת שָׁלוֹם?

Go back to page 91 and practice the שָׁלוֹם רָב before you work on this page.

The Same Ending

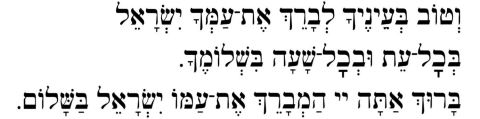

וְטוֹב בְּעֵינֶיךָ לְבָרֵךְ אֶת־עַמְּךָ יִשְׂרָאֵל
בְּכָל־עֵת וּבְכָל־שָׁעָה בִּשְׁלוֹמֶךָ.
בָּרוּךְ אַתָּה יי הַמְבָרֵךְ אֶת־עַמּוֹ יִשְׂרָאֵל בַּשָּׁלוֹם.

Your teacher will help you with your translation.

> My best guess at the meaning of this prayer is:
>
> _____
>
> _____
>
> _____

שָׁלוֹם

To Talk About

A midrash teaches, Whenever God speaks בְּרָכוֹת, prayers, good wishes, and words of comfort to the Families-of-Israel, God's last word is always שָׁלוֹם. When the Messiah comes, he or she will begin with a call for שָׁלוֹם (*Isaiah Rabbah 9.9*).

Questions

1. Where do you go when you want to feel a sense of peace?
2. Where do you go when you want to experience a sense of שָׁלוֹם?

טוֹב

עֵינַיִם

בָּרוּךְ

יִשְׂרָאֵל

שָׁלוֹם

עֲצֹר!

Word Parts		Words	
to/for = לְ	your = ךָ	season = עֵת	nation = עַם
and = וְ/וּ	in/with = בְּ	time = שָׁעָה	all = כָּל

94

עֲשֶׂה שָׁלוֹם

God-Who-Makes-PEACE in the Heavens	1. עֹשֶׂה שָׁלוֹם בִּמְרוֹמָיו
will make PEACE on us	2. הוּא יַעֲשֶׂה שָׁלוֹם עָלֵינוּ
and on all of Israel.	3. וְעַל כָּל-יִשְׂרָאֵל
And we say, Amen.	4. וְאִמְרוּ אָמֵן.

God Buries Truth

Here is a story of God creating peace in the heavens above.

When the Holy One was ready to create people, the ministering angels divided into groups and political parties. One side said, Let people be created, while the other said, Let them not be created.

Love said, Create people because they will perform acts of love.

Truth said, Don't create people because they will all lie a lot.

Righteousness said, Create people because they will do righteous deeds.

Peace said, Don't create people because they will get into conflict after conflict.

What did the Holy One do? God took truth and buried it in the ground. Then God created people. With truth buried, peace was possible (*Genesis Rabbah* 8.5).

Questions
1. What does this story teach about the process of making peace?
2. Why does one need to bury truth in order to make peace?
3. How can knowing this story help us to know where to point our hearts when we say בִּרְכַּת שָׁלוֹם?

Can you see the three letters עשה in these words?
Sometimes the ה drops out.

מַעֲשֶׂיךָ   יַעֲשֶׂה   עוֹשֶׂה

make = עוֹשֶׂה

will make = יַעֲשֶׂה

your makings = מַעֲשֶׂיךָ

Practice these phrases and circle all the words that contain the root עשה.

1. שֶׁעָשַׂנִי בְּצַלְמוֹ   הוּא יַעֲשֶׂה שָׁלוֹם עָלֵינוּ   עֹשֶׂה שָׁלוֹם בִּמְרוֹמָיו

2. שֶׁעָשָׂה נִסִּים   כֻּלָּם בְּחָכְמָה עָשִׂיתָ   מָה רַבּוּ מַעֲשֶׂיךָ יי

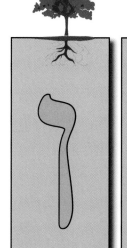
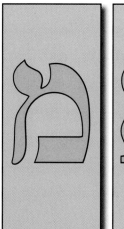

Can you see the three letters אמן in these words?

נֶאֱמָן   אֱמוּנָה   אָמֵן

Hebrew builds words out of three-letter roots.

So be it! = אָמֵן

faith = אֱמוּנָה

faithful = נֶאֱמָן

Practice these phrases and circle all the words that contain the root אמן.

3. וּבִזְמַן קָרִיב וְנֹאמַר אָמֵן   הָאֵל הַנֶּאֱמָן הָאוֹמֵר וְעֹשֶׂה

4. וּמְקַיֵּם אֱמוּנָתוֹ לִישֵׁנֵי עָפָר   יי אֱלֹהִים וְנֶאֱמָנִים דְּבָרֶיךָ

96

עֹשֶׂה

שָׁלוֹם

עַל

יִשְׂרָאֵל

אָמֵן

Word Parts

in/with = בְּ

and = וְ

Words

in the = בִּמְרוֹמָיו
heavens

He = הוּא

all = כָּל

and let = וְאִמְרוּ
us say

Your teacher will help you with your translation.

עֹשֶׂה שָׁלוֹם בִּמְרוֹמָיו
הוּא יַעֲשֶׂה שָׁלוֹם עָלֵינוּ
וְעַל כָּל־יִשְׂרָאֵל וְאִמְרוּ אָמֵן.

My best guess at the meaning of this prayer is:

_____

_____

_____

Choreography

At the end of the עֲמִידָה, during the saying of עֹשֶׂה שָׁלוֹם, a person:

takes three steps backwards

bows to the left (saying,
עֹשֶׂה שָׁלוֹם בִּמְרוֹמָיו)

bows to the right (saying,
הוּא יַעֲשֶׂה שָׁלוֹם עָלֵינוּ)

bows forward (saying,
וְעַל כָּל־יִשְׂרָאֵל וְאִמְרוּ אָמֵן)

pauses for a moment before moving away.

When we take three steps backward we are like:

a servant leaving a master or a citizen backing away from a monarch (*O.H.* 123.1).

Moses leaving Mt. Sinai and going back through the cloud, the fog, and the darkness (*Deut* 4.11). Moses leaving the burning bush and stepping back from the holy space. (*Shibbolei ha-Leket*).

the כֹּהֲנִים leaving the altar where they brought the people's message to God. There were three rows of stones that they stepped over (*Rav Hai Gaon*).

the wicked King Nebuchadnezzar, who took three steps toward God and was rewarded with the victory that destroyed the Temple. If three steps could work for him, they could work for us, too (*Mishnah Brurah* 123.2).

When we bow to the right, left and forward we are acting out a scene.

The angel Mikha'el stands to the right of God. He represents God, the strict judge Who follows all the rules.

The angel Gavri'el stands to the left of God. He speaks for God's commitment to mercy forgiving people and meeting their needs.

The Holy One, is in the middle. God balances justice and mercy to fit every situation. The עֲמִידָה is a moment of judgment we are asking God to balance justice and mercy and fulfill our needs (*Bet Yosef* 123; *Rabbi Eli Munk*).

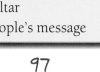

Reviewing בִּרְכַּת שָׁלוֹם

Some things to know about בִּרְכַּת שָׁלוֹם:

בִּרְכַּת שָׁלוֹם is the last בְּרָכָה in the עֲמִידָה. It is the end of the last three "thanksgiving" בְּרָכוֹת.

In Ashkenazic tradition there are two different בְּרָכוֹת. In the morning there is שִׂים שָׁלוֹם. In the afternoon and evening there is שָׁלוֹם רָב.

בִּרְכַּת שָׁלוֹם is based on the priestly benediction.

בִּרְכַּת שָׁלוֹם is about various kinds of peace inner-peace, family peace, and political (world) peace.

שָׁלוֹם is the "end of all blessings."

Language Learning

Roots:

Key Parts

First line שִׂים שָׁלוֹם

שִׂים שָׁלוֹם טוֹבָה וּבְרָכָה חֵן וָחֶסֶד וְרַחֲמִים עָלֵינוּ וְעַל כָּל־יִשְׂרָאֵל עַמֶּךְ

First line שָׁלוֹם רָב

שָׁלוֹם רָב עַל יִשְׂרָאֵל עַמְּךָ תָּשִׂים לְעוֹלָם.

Ending of Both בְּרָכוֹת

וְטוֹב בְּעֵינֶיךָ לְבָרֵךְ אֶת עַמְּךָ יִשְׂרָאֵל בְּכָל־עֵת וּבְכָל־שָׁעָה בִּשְׁלוֹמֶךָ.

בָּרוּךְ אַתָּה יי הַמְבָרֵךְ אֶת־עַמּוֹ יִשְׂרָאֵל בַּשָּׁלוֹם.

עֹשֶׂה שָׁלוֹם

עֹשֶׂה שָׁלוֹם בִּמְרוֹמָיו הוּא יַעֲשֶׂה שָׁלוֹם עָלֵינוּ וְעַל כָּל־יִשְׂרָאֵל וְאִמְרוּ אָמֵן.

עֲצֹר!

98

Unit 9

הַלֵּל

The הַלֵּל is:

a collection of six psalms: 113-118. The Jewish tradition remembers that King David wrote the Psalms.

said on the three festivals: Pesaḥ, Shavuot, and Sukkot. It is also said on Ḥanukkah (but not Purim), and most Jews also say it on Yom ha-Atzma'ut (Israel's Independence Day) and Yom Yerushalayim (Jerusalem Day).

also said as part of the Passover Seder.

the oldest part of the siddur a cycle of prayers that goes all the way back into the service in the Temple.

a group of psalms with really good melodies that are a lot of fun to sing.

The Talmud (*Pesaḥim* 117a-118a) helps us understand the הַלֵּל. It teaches that:

הַלֵּל is said when Israel is in danger and הַלֵּל is said when Israel has been rescued. This teaches us that we can call on God when we need help because God has been there for us in the past when we have needed help.

הַלֵּל traces the history of the Jewish people. It has five themes: (1) the Exodus from Egypt, (2) the crossing of the Reed Sea, (3) the giving of the Torah, (4) the giving of Eternal Life, (5) the coming of the Messiah.

we cannot change the order of the הַלֵּל because it tells a story that starts in the past, leads to the present, and has faith in the future. We believe that God will take care of us because God has taken care of us in the past.

In this unit you will learn:
• about הַלֵּל
• parts of הַלֵּל
• the roots יצא הלל
• הַלֵּל stories mainly connect to King David

הַלֵּל

1. Praised are You, ADONAI our God, Ruler of the Cosmos	בָּרוּךְ אַתָּה יי אֱלֹהֵינוּ מֶלֶךְ הָעוֹלָם
2. Who made us HOLY with the MITZVOT	אֲשֶׁר קִדְּשָׁנוּ בְּמִצְוֹתָיו
2. and made it a MITZVAH for us	וְצִוָּנוּ
3. to read the HALLEL.	לִקְרֹא אֶת-הַהַלֵּל.

Psalm 113

5. HALLELUYAH (Sing praise to God)	הַלְלוּיָהּ.
6. HALLELU (Sing praise) God's workers	הַלְלוּ עַבְדֵי יי
7. HALLELU God's name	הַלְלוּ אֶת-שֵׁם יי
8. Let God's name be BLESSED	יְהִי שֵׁם יי מְבֹרָךְ
9. from now and beyond forever.	מֵעַתָּה וְעַד עוֹלָם....

Psalm 114

10. When Israel went out of Egypt	בְּצֵאת יִשְׂרָאֵל מִמִּצְרָיִם
11. The House of Jacob	בֵּית יַעֲקֹב
11. went from being a nation with a strange tongue	מֵעַם לֹעֵז.
12. Judah became God's Holy One	הָיְתָה יְהוּדָה לְקָדְשׁוֹ
13. Israel became God's domain.	יִשְׂרָאֵל מַמְשְׁלוֹתָיו.
14. The sea saw it and fled,	הַיָּם רָאָה וַיָּנֹס
15. the Jordan turned backwards.	הַיַּרְדֵּן יִסֹּב לְאָחוֹר.
16. The mountains leaped like rams,	הֶהָרִים רָקְדוּ כְאֵילִים
17. the hills (leaped) like young sheep.	גְּבָעוֹת כִּבְנֵי צֹאן.
18. What's with you sea that you flee?	מַה לְּךָ הַיָּם כִּי תָנוּס
19. Jordan why do you turn backwards?	הַיַּרְדֵּן תִּסֹּב לְאָחוֹר.

Choreography

הַלֵּל is said (and mainly sung) standing. We stand because we are testifying. In ancient times, witnesses in a court stood.

Mountains why do you leap like rams?	20. הֶהָרִים תִּרְקְדוּ כְאֵילִים
Hills why (leap) like lambs?	21. גְּבָעוֹת כִּבְנֵי-צֹאן.
The earth quakes at the presence of the Master	22. מִלִּפְנֵי אָדוֹן חוּלִי אָרֶץ
at the presence of the God of Jacob.	23. מִלִּפְנֵי אֱלוֹהַ יַעֲקֹב,
The One who turned the rock into a pool of water,	21. הַהֹפְכִי הַצּוּר אֲגַם מָיִם
Turned the flint into a fountain of water.	22. חַלָּמִישׁ לְמַעְיְנוֹ מָיִם.

Psalm 118:19-20

Open the gates of righteousness for me	23. פִּתְחוּ לִי שַׁעֲרֵי צֶדֶק
I will come in and give thanks to God	24. אָבֹא בָם אוֹדֶה יָהּ.
This is ADONAI's gate,	25. זֶה הַשַּׁעַר לַיְיָ
the righteous will come in through it…	26. צַדִּיקִים יָבֹאוּ בוֹ...

Psalm 118:25

Please ADONAI save us!	27. אָנָּא יי הוֹשִׁיעָה נָּא.
Please ADONAI save us!	28. אָנָּא יי הוֹשִׁיעָה נָּא.
Please ADONAI give us success!	29. אָנָּא יי הַצְלִיחָה נָּא.
Please ADONAI give us success!	30. אָנָּא יי הַצְלִיחָה נָּא.

There are many traditions about the times that הַלֵּל was first said. These include: (a) Moses and Israel sang it when they came out of the Reed Sea. (b) Joshua sang it when the Canaanites threatened the people. (c) Deborah and Barak sang it when they faced Sisera. (d) Hezekiah sang it when Jerusalem was attacked by Assyria. (e) Ḥananiah, Misha'el, and Azariah sang it when Nebuchadnezzar threatened them. (f) Esther and Mordechai sang it when Haman wanted to destroy the Jews (*Pesahim 117a*). How can all of these moments be the first time? When else in Jewish history would be a good הַלֵּל-saying moment?

On the last six days of Passover we say only a shortened הַלֵּל. A midrash explains why. After Israel crossed the Reed Sea safely they started singing הַלֵּל. The angels joined in. God yelled at the angels, How can you sing when my creations are drowning? The angels stopped. During the seder we take drops of wine out of our Kiddush cup when we remember the suffering of the Egyptians during the plagues. We shorten the הַלֵּל on Passover for the same reason. How can we both celebrate and feel bad about the same victory?

Here is a chance to review the root הָלֵל.

הַלֵּל   יְהַלְלוּ   הַלְלוּיָה

Prayers of Praise = הַלֵּל

Let us praise = יְהַלְלוּ

Praise the Eternal! = הַלְלוּיָה

Practice these phrases and circle all the words that contain the root הָלֵל.

1. הַלְלוּ עַבְדֵי יי הַלְלוּ אֶת־שֵׁם יי   כֹּל הַנְּשָׁמָה תְּהַלֵּל יָה הַלְלוּיָה

2. הַלְלוּהוּ בְּתֵקַע שׁוֹפָר   מֶלֶךְ מְהֻלָּל בַּתִּשְׁבָּחוֹת

mitzvah
צִוָּה

קָדוֹשׁ

עוֹלָם

מֶלֶךְ

אַתָּה

בָּרוּךְ

קָרָא

הָלֵל
Words

Who = אֲשֶׁר

Your teacher will help you with your translation.

בָּרוּךְ אַתָּה יי אֱלֹהֵינוּ מֶלֶךְ הָעוֹלָם
אֲשֶׁר קִדְּשָׁנוּ בְּמִצְוֹתָיו וְצִוָּנוּ לִקְרֹא אֶת־הַהַלֵּל.

My best guess at the meaning of this prayer is:

_____

_____

_____

David and the Spider

When David was a boy he ran into a web and he got got mad at a spider for making it. He asked God, Why did You ever create something as useless as spiders?

David wound up working for King Saul. When David was a boy he ran an errand for his father. His older brothers were soldiers. He showed up in the camp at the right moment. David faced the giant Goliath with his slingshot when everyone else chickened out. After his victory he became an important member of Saul's court. He grew up and scored a lot more victories. The king became jealous of David and tried to kill him. David fled, and Saul declared him a criminal and started to chase him with his army. David hid in a cave and fell asleep. While he slept, a spider wove a thick web at the cave's entrance. David woke up just before Saul and his soldiers showed up there. Saul saw the spiderweb and said, He couldn't be in here. This web saved David, who then sang a piece of הַלֵּל, You who believe in the Eternal trust in the Eternal. God is their help and shield (*Alphabet of Ben Sira* 24b).

עֲצֹר!

Questions

1. What can you learn from this story?
2. How did God save David from King Saul?
3. How can knowing this story help you know where to point your heart when you say the הַלֵּל?

Practice Psalm 113.

1. הַלְלוּיָהּ

2. הַלְלוּ אֶת־שֵׁם יי   הַלְלוּ עַבְדֵי יי

3. מֵעַתָּה וְעַד עוֹלָם   יְהִי שֵׁם יי מְבֹרָךְ

4. מְהֻלָּל שֵׁם יי   מִמִּזְרַח־שֶׁמֶשׁ עַד מְבוֹאוֹ

5. עַל הַשָּׁמַיִם כְּבוֹדוֹ   רָם עַל כָּל־גּוֹיִם יי

6. הַמַּגְבִּיהִי לָשָׁבֶת   מִי כַּיי אֱלֹהֵינוּ

7. בַּשָּׁמַיִם וּבָאָרֶץ   הַמַּשְׁפִּילִי לִרְאוֹת

8. מֵאַשְׁפֹּת יָרִים אֶבְיוֹן   מְקִימִי מֵעָפָר דָּל

9. עִם נְדִיבֵי עַמּוֹ   לְהוֹשִׁיבִי עִם נְדִיבִים

10. אֵם הַבָּנִים שְׂמֵחָה.   מוֹשִׁיבִי עֲקֶרֶת הַבַּיִת

11. הַלְלוּיָהּ.

הַלֵּל

בָּרוּךְ

Your teacher will help you with your translation.

Psalm 113

הַלְלוּיָהּ.
הַלְלוּ עַבְדֵי יי, הַלְלוּ אֶת-שֵׁם יי
יְהִי שֵׁם יי מְבֹרָךְ מֵעַתָּה וְעַד עוֹלָם.

My best guess at the meaning of this psalm is:

_____

_____

_____

_____

עוֹלָם

Words

עַבְדֵי = workers of

יְהִי = let

שֵׁם = name

עַתָּה = now

עַד = until

Word Parts

מֵ = from

וְ = and

To Talk About

One strange thing about this psalm is that it talks about God's Name and not God. The Dubner Maggid told this story to explain why.

Once there was a queen with a huge empire it was too big for her to visit every place. One day an imper-sonator dressed up like a queen and visited a part of the empire where the real queen had never been. The people all treated her warmly with great respect and honor.

When the real queen heard about this everyone expected her to be angry, but she wasn't. They thought that she would punish the people for worshipping the wrong queen, but she said, They thought that they were honoring me, not the imposter. They just need to be introduced to the real me.

The Dubner Maggid explained, Many different people see the things that God does in the world, but not all of them figure out which Power was responsible. God says the same thing as the queen. 'They need to learn My Name. They need to be introduced to the real Me' (Rabbi Abraham J. Twerski, *Prayerfully Yours*).

Why does the psalmist talk about God's Name and not just God ?

Can you see the three letters **יצא** in these words?

Sometimes the **י** drops out.

הַמּוֹצִיא בְּצֵאת יָצָא

left = יָצָא

when leaving = בְּצֵאת

the one who takes out = הַמּוֹצִיא

Practice these phrases and circle all the words that contain the root **יצא**.

1. בְּצֵאת יִשְׂרָאֵל מִמִּצְרָיִם   כִּי מִצִּיּוֹן תֵּצֵא תוֹרָה וּדְבַר יי מִירוּשָׁלָיִם

2. הַמּוֹצִיא לֶחֶם מִן הָאָרֶץ   אֲשֶׁר הוֹצֵאתִי אֶתְכֶם מֵאֶרֶץ מִצְרָיִם

Leaving Egypt

In Hebrew the Exodus from Egypt is called יְצִיאַת מִצְרָיִם.
מִצְרָיִם is the Hebrew word for Egypt. It is built around
the three- letter root [מצר]. A מֵצַר is a pit. מְצָרִים is
plural. That makes Egypt the pits. The word מֵצַר is built
out of the two letters צַר, which means narrowness. A
rabbi named the Sefat Emet taught, We each have our
own Egypt, our own 'narrowness,' that we have to escape.

Another rabbi, Isaac of Gur, taught the same lesson in
a different way. He said, In every generation there is a
new understanding of leaving Egypt. Egypt is inside
of us. We all have our own Pharaohs. Not only in
every generation, but in every person there is a point of
freedom. To touch that point is to exit the inner Egypt.
That point can only be found individually by each person.

Explain the idea of a personal Egypt in your own words.

_____

_____

_____

106

Psalm 114

בְּצֵאת יִשְׂרָאֵל מִמִּצְרַיִם בֵּית יַעֲקֹב מֵעַם לֹעֵז.

יָצָא

יִשְׂרָאֵל

מִצְרַיִם

בֵּית

יַעֲקֹב

עֲצֹר!

Your teacher will help you with your translation.

My best guess at the meaning of this prayer is:

_____

_____

_____

Words

nation = עַם

strange language = לֹעֵז

Word Parts

from = מִ/מֵ

To Talk About

There are two stories about the first time that בְּצֵאת יִשְׂרָאֵל was sung. One version says that Israel sang it once they successfully crossed the Reed Sea (and while the Egyptians were drowning).

The other says that King David was studying about יְצִיאַת מִצְרַיִם. David learned that there were many reasons that God found the Families-of-Israel to be worth saving. There were four: (1) They kept their Hebrew names, (2) they did not give up Hebrew as their language, (3) they did not tell each others' secrets, and (4) husbands and wives were good to their partners. And there were some more reasons: because they celebrated a Passover on their last night in Egypt, because they passed the Covenant with God onto their children, and because in the future they would accept the Torah and would build the Tabernacle. When David learned about all of these good things that Israel did because of their faith in God, he just had to sing. Out came בְּצֵאת יִשְׂרָאֵל (Midrash Tehillim 114.4).

Can both of these stories be true? What can we learn from each one?

Can you see the three letters צדק in these words?

צְדָקָה צַדִּיק צֶדֶק

Hebrew builds words out of three-letter roots.

justice = צֶדֶק

righteous person = צַדִּיק

charity = צְדָקָה

Practice these phrases and circle all the words that contain the root צדק.

1. צַדִּיק כַּתָּמָר יִפְרָח כְּאֶרֶז בַּלְּבָנוֹן יִשְׂגֶּה

2. מִשְׁפְּטֵי יי אֱמֶת, צָדְקוּ יַחְדָּו

3. צִדְקָתְךָ צֶדֶק הָעוֹלָם וְתוֹרָתְךָ אֱמֶת

4. פִּתְחוּ לִי שַׁעֲרֵי צֶדֶק אָבֹא בָם אוֹדֶה יָהּ

5. וּתְשׁוּבָה וּתְפִלָּה וּצְדָקָה מַעֲבִירִין אֶת־רֹעַ הַגְּזֵרָה

6. זֵכֶר רַב־טוּבְךָ יַבִּיעוּ וְצִדְקָתְךָ יְרַנֵּנוּ

7. צַדִּיק יי בְּכָל־דְּרָכָיו וְחָסִיד בְּכָל־מַעֲשָׂיו

8. וְעַל הַצַּדִּיקִים וְעַל הַחֲסִידִים וְעַל זִקְנֵי עַמְּךָ בֵּית יִשְׂרָאֵל

Write in the missing letters for these words that are built from the root צדק.

11. צְ__קָה   10. __דֶק   9. צַדִּי__

Psalm 118

Your teacher will help you with your translation.

פִּתְחוּ לִי שַׁעֲרֵי צֶדֶק, אָבֹא בָם, אוֹדֶה יָהּ.
זֶה הַשַּׁעַר לַיי, צַדִּיקִים יָבֹאוּ בוֹ.

My best guess at the meaning of this psalm is:

_____

_____

_____

_____

פָּתַח

שַׁעַר

צֶדֶק

Words

I will come = אָבֹא

in them = בָם

I will thank = אוֹדֶה

God = יָהּ

this = זֶה

in it = בוֹ

Word Parts

to/for = לְ

for me = לִי

To Talk About

One big question about this psalm is What gates are we talking about? Rashi, a famous medieval biblical commentator, said, This is a dream of the future. In the future, after the Messiah comes, the Temple will be rebuilt in Jerusalem. In that Messianic future, all good people will gather and enter and come close to each other and to God.

Rashi lived around the year 1000. Today, not all Jews believe that it would be wonderful to rebuild the Temple. So Rashi's comment could be understood to mean the gates to a time when all people live in peace, safety, and prosperity.

This is just one interpretation of שַׁעֲרֵי צֶדֶק. You will see another interpretation on page 111. What do you think Gates of Righteousness means?

please · save us · Adonai · I beg of you

אָנָּא יי הוֹשִׁיעָה נָא.

please · _____ · Adonai · I beg of you

אָנָּא יי הוֹשִׁיעָה נָא.

please · give us good fortune · Adonai · _____

אָנָּא יי הַצְלִיחָה נָא.

please · _____ · Adonai · I beg of you

אָנָּא יי הַצְלִיחָה נָא.

Your teacher will help you with your translation.

My best guess at the purpose of this prayer is:

_____

_____

_____

To Talk About

Starting a few lines before the אָנָּא יי we begin singing Psalm 118 differently. First, the service leader sings a verse, then the whole congregation repeats it. Every time we sing a Hebrew prayer responsively (back and forth between the service leader and the congregation) we are acting out a story.

According to the Talmud (*Pesaḥim* 119a) these words were first said by Samuel, the prophet, when he came looking for a king. David, his brothers, and his father, Jesse, all echoed Samuel's words because they were in shock. They didn't believe God would want David. He was the youngest and scrawniest of the brothers.

When David was finally appointed king, he realized two things. Just as God had saved him from Goliath, Saul, and the Philistines and brought him to this great moment of his becoming king, so God had taken Israel out of slavery, protected them in the wilderness, and brought them into the promised land. David knew that God could be counted on for help. That is why we ask God for help just as David did.

In what one way is your life story like the story of the Families-of-Israel?

King David Learns about the Meaning of Life

A midrash teaches:

King David learned that when a person is ready to enter the life after this life, she will be asked, What was your work? If she answers, I fed the hungry, they will say to her, This is God's gate, and let her in. If he answers, I gave drink to those who are thirsty, they will say to him, This is God's gate, and let him in. If she answers, I gave clothes to those who need them, they will say to her, This is God's gate, and let her in. If he answers, I took care of orphans, gave tzedakah, or performed other deeds of lovingkindness, the same will happen. David said, I do all of these things, so let all the gates be opened for me. He then wrote, פִּתְחוּ לִי שַׁעֲרֵי צֶדֶק.

Questions

1. According to this midrash, what are the Gates of Righteousness? What does it take to open them?
2. The הַלֵּל starts with the Exodus from Egypt, moves on to crossing the Reed Sea, and then takes us to Mount Sinai. How is this psalm connected to those events?
3. In the Talmud we are told about a number of "spiritual gates", the Gates of Prayer, the Gates of Weeping, the Gates of Repentance, the Gates of Paradise, and the Gates of Wounded Feelings. What other unique gates may there be?
4. How does knowing this story of David help you know where to point your heart when you say this part of הַלֵּל?

111

Have Faith

A woman came to the Tzadik of Sanz and complained about God. She said that her life was too hard. The Tzadik told her, Have faith in God and God will take care of you. She said to the Tzadik, The siddur says it works the other way. There it says that God saved the Jews in Egypt. When they saw the great miracles, then they believed in God. The Tzadik smiled and said, You are right. First God will help you then your faith will grow (Rabbi Abraham J. Twerski, *Not Just Stories*).

Questions

1. Do you agree with the rabbi or the woman?
2. How is this story a הַלֵּל story?

Reviewing הַלֵּל

Some things to know about הַלֵּל

הַלֵּל is a collection of six psalms (113-118) that were originally sung in the Temple in Jerusalem.

הַלֵּל has two stories. One comes from Israel crossing the Reed Sea. The other comes from King David.

הַלֵּל is said on the three festivals: Pesah, Shavuot, and Sukkot. It is also said on Hanukkah (but not Purim) and most Jews also say it on Yom ha-Atzma'ut (Israel's Independence Day) and Yom Yerushalayim (Jerusalem Day).

הַלֵּל is also part of the Passover Seder.

Through celebrating times when God has saved and rescued the Jewish people we build our faith and understanding that God will be there to rescue us.

Language Learning

Roots:

The Heart of the Prayer

The central moment of הַלֵּל is probably the story the Exodus:

בְּצֵאת יִשְׂרָאֵל מִמִּצְרָיִם בֵּית יַעֲקֹב מֵעַם לֹעֵז.

It ends with a direct request to God to be our helper.

אָנָּא יי הוֹשִׁיעָה נָא. אָנָּא יי הַצְלִיחָה נָא

לְכָה דוֹדִי

קַבָּלַת שַׁבָּת

On Friday night we have a very short service that is unlike any other service. It happens just before the evening service. It is called קַבָּלַת שַׁבָּת, The Welcoming of Shabbat. The service was created in the sixteenth century in the Israeli city of Tzfat.

The Talmud

In the Talmud we are told that Rabbi Hanina would put on his best clothes, go outside and watch the sunset on עֶרֶב שַׁבָּת (Friday night). He would sing Come, let us go out and welcome Shabbat the Queen. Rabbi Yannai would do exactly the same thing, except he would sing, Come, O Bride; come, O Bride!

Kabbalists

In 1492 Jews began leaving Spain, Italy and other places in Europe because they were not allowed to practice their religion and live in peace. One of the places they gathered was the city of Tzfat. The city became a magnet for Kabbalists, Jewish mystics. These scholars created a service out of the Talmudic description of Rabbi Hanina and Rabbi Yannai going out to welcome שַׁבָּת.

לְכָה דוֹדִי

Rabbi Shlomo Ha-Levy, a Kabbalist from Tzfat, wrote a song to use at this service. It is לְכָה דוֹדִי.

Some things to know about לְכָה דוֹדִי:

It has nine verses; eight of them spell out Shlomo ha-Levy's name in the first letter of each verse.

It calls שַׁבָּת both a queen and a bride.

It talks about three things: Shabbat, Jerusalem, and the Redemption. (The Redemption is when God finally helps us to fix the world and make it into a place that is good for everyone.)

In this unit you will learn:
• about לְכָה דוֹדִי
בוֹא זֵכֶר שָׁמֹר
• three "big ideas" found in לְכָה דוֹדִי

לְכָה דוֹדִי

1. Come my friend let's greet the BRIDE	לְכָה דוֹדִי לִקְרַאת כַּלָּה
2. Let us welcome the face of SHABBAT.	פְּנֵי שַׁבָּת נְקַבְּלָה.
3. "GUARD" and "REMEMBER" are said as ONE	שָׁמוֹר וְזָכוֹר בְּדִבּוּר אֶחָד
4. we are able to hear them together because of a UNIFYING God	הִשְׁמִיעָנוּ אֵל הַמְיֻחָד.
5. ADONAI is ONE and God's NAME is ONE.	יי אֶחָד וּשְׁמוֹ אֶחָד
6. This all goes to NAME, BEAUTY, and PRAISE.	לְשֵׁם וּלְתִפְאֶרֶת וְלִתְהִלָּה.
7. To greet SHABBAT let us go	לִקְרַאת שַׁבָּת לְכוּ וְנֵלְכָה
8. because She is a SOURCE of BLESSING.	כִּי הִיא מְקוֹר הַבְּרָכָה.
9. from the BEGINNING, from BEFORE, She was appointed—	מֵרֹאשׁ מִקֶּדֶם נְסוּכָה
10. the FINAL CREATION was in the THOUGHT that came First.	סוֹף מַעֲשֶׂה בְּמַחֲשָׁבָה תְּחִלָּה.
11. Sanctuary of the RULER, RULING city,	מִקְדַּשׁ מֶלֶךְ עִיר מְלוּכָה,
12. GET yourself UP, leave your desolation.	קוּמִי צְאִי מִתּוֹךְ הַהֲפֵכָה.
13. It is too much for You to sit in a valley of tears	רַב לָךְ שֶׁבֶת בְּעֵמֶק הַבָּכָא,
14. God will act with compassion for you.	וְהוּא יַחֲמוֹל עָלַיִךְ חֶמְלָה.
15. SHAKE it off. GET UP from the dust.	הִתְנַעֲרִי, מֵעָפָר קוּמִי,
16. Put on garments of beauty, my people.	לִבְשִׁי בִּגְדֵי תִפְאַרְתֵּךְ עַמִּי.
17. Soon comes the son of Jesse from Bethlehem—	עַל יַד בֶּן־יִשַׁי בֵּית הַלַּחְמִי.
18. and near to my soul is redemption.	קָרְבָה אֶל נַפְשִׁי גְאָלָהּ.
19. WAKE UP. WAKE UP,	הִתְעוֹרְרִי הִתְעוֹרְרִי
20. because your LIGHT is coming. GET UP and SHINE.	כִּי בָא אוֹרֵךְ קוּמִי אוֹרִי.
21. WAKE. WAKE. Sing my song!	עוּרִי עוּרִי שִׁיר דַּבֵּרִי,
22. ADONAI's honor is revealed in you.	כְּבוֹד יי עָלַיִךְ נִגְלָה.

Don't be ashamed. Don't be humiliated.	לֹא תֵבֹשִׁי וְלֹא תִכָּלְמִי, 23.
Why are you down? Why are you depressed?	מַה תִּשְׁתּוֹחֲחִי וּמַה תֶּהֱמִי. 24.
You will shelter the poor of my people.	בָּךְ יֶחֱסוּ עֲנִיֵּי עַמִּי, 25.
You will be REBUILT out of the RUINS.	וְנִבְנְתָה עִיר עַל תִּלָּהּ. 26.
Then your destroyers will be destroyed	וְהָיוּ לִמְשִׁסָּה שֹׁאסָיִךְ 27.
Those who devoured you will be exiled far away.	וְרָחֲקוּ כָּל־מְבַלְּעָיִךְ. 28.
Your God will REJOICE over you	יָשִׂישׂ עָלַיִךְ אֱלֹהָיִךְ 29.
Like a groom REJOICES over a BRIDE.	כִּמְשׂוֹשׂ חָתָן עַל כַּלָּה. 30.
Right and left you will SPREAD OUT	יָמִין וּשְׂמֹאל תִּפְרֹצִי 31.
And before GOD TREMBLE.	וְאֶת־יְיָ תַּעֲרִיצִי. 32.
Through a family that started with Peretz (David's family)	עַל יַד אִישׁ בֶּן־פַּרְצִי, 33.
We shall be glad and happy.	וְנִשְׂמְחָה וְנָגִילָה. 34.
Enter in PEACE, Crown of her partner	בּוֹאִי בְשָׁלוֹם עֲטֶרֶת בַּעְלָהּ, 35.
With JOY and with GLADNESS	גַּם בְּשִׂמְחָה וּבְצָהֳלָה, 36.
In the midst of the BELIEVERS of a TREASURED PEOPLE	תּוֹךְ אֱמוּנֵי עַם סְגֻלָּה, 37.
COME BRIDE. COME BRIDE.	בּוֹאִי כַלָּה, בּוֹאִי כַלָּה. 38.

שַׁבָּת the Bride

In the midrash we are told this story. שַׁבָּת went crying to God, saying, I am all alone. She explained, Every other day of the week has its own partner. Sunday has Monday. Tuesday has Wednesday. Thursday has Friday. I am the only one who is alone. God said to her, Don't worry. The Families-of-Israel will be your partner (*Genesis R.* 11.8).

The idea of שַׁבָּת as a bride comes from this story. How can the community of Israel and a day of week be partners?

Ahad ha-Am was a Zionist thinker who helped the modern State of Israel come to be. He taught, More than Israel has kept שַׁבָּת, שַׁבָּת has kept Israel. What does it mean to keep שַׁבָּת? How does שַׁבָּת keep Israel?

The Structure of לְכָה דוֹדִי

Verses one and two talk about שַׁבָּת. Verses three to eight talk about Jerusalem being rebuilt. Verse eight adds the Messiah to this story. Verse nine brings us back to שַׁבָּת.

There is a teaching in the Talmud: Three things give us an advance sense of what the *Olam ha-Ba* (world to come) is like. They are שַׁבָּת, sunshine, and wonderful smells (*Brakhot* 57b). How do the images of Jerusalem being rebuilt and the Messiah coming connect to שַׁבָּת as a foretaste of the *Olam ha-Ba"*?

And because they are wonderful questions: How is שַׁבָּת like sunshine? How is שַׁבָּת like a wonderful smell?

Secret Code: Can you find the hidden name of the author, שְׁלֹמֹה הַלֵוִי?

The Chorus of לְכָה דוֹדִי

Your teacher will help you with your translation.

לְכָה דוֹדִי לִקְרַאת כַּלָה
פְּנֵי שַׁבָּת נְקַבְּלָה.

My best guess at the meaning of this prayer is:

_____

_____

_____

לְכָה

כַּלָה

פָּנִים

שַׁבָּת

Words

דוֹדִי = my friend

לִקְרַאת = to greet

נְקַבְּלָה = we will welcome

To Talk About

One really big idea about שַׁבָּת is that in its שָׁלוֹם, things that have been far apart can come back together again. Remember, שָׁלוֹם really means *whole* or *together*.

When we make שַׁבָּת at home, families that have drifted away from each other in the week's business can have a new sense of שָׁלוֹם (coming close again). Especially if two family members have been arguing, שַׁבָּת is a perfect way to feel שָׁלוֹם again.

We are taught that the same is true of God and Israel. At times we can be far apart. When we welcome the שַׁבָּת Queen into our house and our community, we are really inviting God in.

We are told in the Talmud that God often avoids places with sadness but comes close to a person who in the middle of the joy of doing a mitzvah (*Shabbat* 30b).

Questions: How can welcoming Shabbat bring God into your home? What things can you do to make שַׁבָּת a strong invitation to God?

Shabbat Starts with a Sigh

Rabbi <u>H</u>anokh of Alexander told this story. "When I first became a rabbi this happened in my synagogue. A butcher was working and working. He didn't stop on Friday afternoon to get ready for Shabbat. He kept on chopping and chopping meat. Suddenly, he realized that it might already be Shabbat. He was afraid that he had broken the Torah's rule and been working on the Sabbath. He ran directly to the synagogue. He didn't even take off his bloody apron. He burst through the doors and heard the first words of לְכָה דוֹדִי. He had just made it. He sighed a big sigh of relief. At that moment, the sigh that came out of his mouth was the sigh of all the Jews who were in Egypt. They sighed to God out of their bondage. They, too, stopped their labor when Shabbat came."

(Martin Buber, *Tales of the <u>H</u>asidim, Later Masters*)

Questions

1. How could the sigh of thousands of Jews in Egypt come out of a Polish butcher's mouth?
2. What does this story teach us about the importance of קַבָּלַת שַׁבָּת (welcoming Shabbat)?
3. How can knowing this story help you know where to point your heart when you say לְכָה דוֹדִי?

Vocabulary Game

Play a game with some of the vocabulary words you have learned. You know, "I'll take the קְדוּשָׁה for 300 points."

	הַלֵּל	בִּרְכַּת שָׁלוֹם	קְדוּשָׁה	גְּבוּרוֹת	אָבוֹת אִמָּהוֹת	שְׂפָתַי תִּפְתָּח
100	בְּצֵאת	שָׁלוֹם	קָדוֹשׁ	אַתָּה	שָׂרָה	פֶּה
200	שַׁעַר	טוֹב	מֶלֶךְ	גִּבּוֹר	רָחֵל	פּוֹתֵחַ
300	בַּיִת	יִשְׂרָאֵל	כָּבוֹד	עוֹלָם	אַבְרָהָם	תְּהִלָּה
400	צֶדֶק	עֹשֶׂה	בָּרוּךְ	סוֹמֵךְ	רִבְקָה	הִגִּיד
500	מִצְרַיִם	עֵינַיִם	הַלְלוּיָהּ	אָסוּר	יַעֲקֹב	שְׂפָתַיִם

Practice לְכָה דוֹדִי

Here is the full לְכָה דוֹדִי as it appears in the siddur. You may want to sing as you practice.

לְכָה דוֹדִי לִקְרַאת כַּלָּה פְּנֵי שַׁבָּת נְקַבְּלָה.

1. שָׁמוֹר וְזָכוֹר בְּדִבּוּר אֶחָד הִשְׁמִיעָנוּ אֵל הַמְיֻחָד.
יְיָ אֶחָד וּשְׁמוֹ אֶחָד לְשֵׁם וּלְתִפְאֶרֶת וְלִתְהִלָּה. לְכָה דוֹדִי...

2. לִקְרַאת שַׁבָּת לְכוּ וְנֵלְכָה כִּי הִיא מְקוֹר הַבְּרָכָה.
מֵרֹאשׁ מִקֶּדֶם נְסוּכָה סוֹף מַעֲשֶׂה בְּמַחֲשָׁבָה תְּחִלָּה. לְכָה דוֹדִי...

3. מִקְדַּשׁ מֶלֶךְ עִיר מְלוּכָה, קוּמִי צְאִי מִתּוֹךְ הַהֲפֵכָה.
רַב לָךְ שֶׁבֶת בְּעֵמֶק הַבָּכָא, וְהוּא יַחֲמוֹל עָלַיִךְ חֶמְלָה. לְכָה דוֹדִי...

4. הִתְנַעֲרִי, מֵעָפָר קוּמִי, לִבְשִׁי בִּגְדֵי תִפְאַרְתֵּךְ עַמִּי.
עַל יַד בֶּן־יִשַׁי בֵּית הַלַּחְמִי קָרְבָה אֶל נַפְשִׁי גְאָלָה. לְכָה דוֹדִי...

5. הִתְעוֹרְרִי הִתְעוֹרְרִי כִּי בָא אוֹרֵךְ קוּמִי אוֹרִי.
עוּרִי עוּרִי שִׁיר דַּבֵּרִי, כְּבוֹד יְיָ עָלַיִךְ נִגְלָה. לְכָה דוֹדִי...

6. לֹא תֵבשִׁי וְלֹא תִכָּלְמִי, מַה תִּשְׁתּוֹחֲחִי וּמַה תֶּהֱמִי.
בָּךְ יֶחֱסוּ עֲנִיֵי עַמִּי, וְנִבְנְתָה עִיר עַל תִּלָּהּ. לְכָה דוֹדִי...

7. וְהָיוּ לִמְשִׁסָּה שׁאסָיִךְ וְרָחֲקוּ כָּל־מְבַלְּעָיִךְ.
יָשִׂישׂ עָלַיִךְ אֱלֹהָיִךְ כִּמְשׂוֹשׂ חָתָן עַל כַּלָּה. לְכָה דוֹדִי...

8. יָמִין וּשְׂמֹאל תִּפְרֹצִי וְאֶת־יְיָ תַּעֲרִיצִי.
עַל יַד אִישׁ בֶּן־פַּרְצִי, וְנִשְׂמְחָה וְנָגִילָה. לְכָה דוֹדִי...

9. בּוֹאִי בְשָׁלוֹם עֲטֶרֶת בַּעְלָהּ, גַּם בְּשִׂמְחָה וּבְצָהֳלָה,
תּוֹךְ אֱמוּנֵי עַם סְגֻלָּה, בּוֹאִי כַלָּה, בּוֹאִי כַלָּה. לְכָה דוֹדִי...

Can you see the three letters שמר in these words?

שׁוֹמְרֵנוּ   וְשָׁמְרוּ   שָׁמוֹר

Hebrew builds words out of three-letter roots.

guard = שָׁמוֹר

and they will guard = וְשָׁמְרוּ

our guard = שׁוֹמְרֵנוּ

Practice these phrases and circle all the words that contain the root שמר.

1. שָׁמוֹר וְזָכוֹר בְּדִבּוּר אֶחָד

כִּי אֵל שׁוֹמְרֵנוּ וּמַצִּילֵנוּ אָתָּה

2. וְשָׁמְרוּ בְנֵי־יִשְׂרָאֵל אֶת־הַשַּׁבָּת

וּשְׁמוֹר צֵאתֵנוּ וּבוֹאֵנוּ לְחַיִּים וּלְשָׁלוֹם

Can you see the three letters זכר in these words?

זֵכֶר   זָכְרֵנוּ   זְכֹר

remember! = זְכֹר

remember us = זָכְרֵנוּ

the memory of = זֵכֶר

Practice these phrases and circle all the words that contain the root זכר.

3. זָכְרֵנוּ לְחַיִּים מֶלֶךְ חָפֵץ בַּחַיִּים

לְמִקְרָאֵי־קֹדֶשׁ זֵכֶר לִיצִיאַת מִצְרַיִם

4. דְּבָרִי בּוֹ זְכֹר אֶזְכְּרֶנוּ עוֹד

בָּרוּךְ אַתָּה יְיָ זוֹכֵר הַבְּרִית

120

Your teacher will help you with your translation.

The First Verse of לְכָה דוֹדִי

שָׁמוֹר וְזָכוֹר בְּדִבּוּר אֶחָד
הִשְׁמִיעָנוּ אֵל הַמְיֻחָד
יְיָ אֶחָד וּשְׁמוֹ אֶחָד
לְשֵׁם וּלְתִפְאֶרֶת וְלִתְהִלָּה.

My best guess at the meaning of this prayer is:

_____

_____

_____

שָׁמוֹר

זָכוֹר

דִּבֶּר

1
אֶחָד

שָׁמַע

הַלֵּל

To Talk About

The Ten Commandments appear twice in the Torah once in the book of Exodus and once in Deuteronomy. These two sets are just about the same except for the Shabbat commandment. One of these commandments begins שָׁמוֹר אֶת־יוֹם הַשַּׁבָּת (Guarding the Sabbath Day) (*Deut.* 5.12) and the other begins זָכוֹר אֶת־יוֹם הַשַּׁבָּת (Remember the Sabbath Day) (*Ex.* 20.8).

In the Talmud (*Sh'vu'ot* 20b) we are told that one of the miracles of Mount Sinai was that God said both שָׁמוֹר and זָכוֹר at the same time. Both ideas were expressed at once.

Rabbi B. Jacobson explains, "זָכוֹר has to do with lighting candles, saying kiddush, and doing things that show that you know it is Shabbat. שָׁמוֹר has to do with not working on Shabbat. It is the things that you stop doing on Shabbat to make it a day of rest" (*The Shabbat Service*).

Word Parts		Words
and = וְ\וּ	for/to = לְ	God = אֵל
in/with = בְּ	His = וֹ	name = שֵׁם
the = הַ		beauty = תִפְאֶרֶת

A Shabbat Memory

Write down a Shabbat memory. It could be from Shabbat at home or at camp. It could be about Shabbat in your synagogue or it could even be a memory from either preparing for Shabbat or learning about Shabbat.

_____

_____

_____

_____

_____

_____

Was this a memory about keeping Shabbat or remembering Shabbat?

_____

זָכוֹר

List three things that a family could do to create a Shabbat that was a wonderful Jewish day of celebration.

_____

_____

_____

שָׁמוֹר

List three things that a family could choose not to do for a day to create a Shabbat that is a real day of rest.

_____

_____

_____

עֲצוֹר!

Go back to pages 114-115 and read the לְכָה דוֹדִי before you work on this page.

Can you see the three letters בוא in these words?

וַהֲבִיאֵנוּ   בּוֹאִי   בּוֹא

בּוֹא = come

בּוֹאִי = come!

וַהֲבִיאֵנוּ = and bring us

Practice these phrases and circle all the words that contain the root בוא.

1. בּוֹאִי כַלָּה בּוֹאִי כַלָּה!   וְיָבוֹא מֶלֶךְ הַכָּבוֹד

2. בּוֹא יָבֹא בְרִנָּה נֹשֵׂא אֲלֻמֹּתָיו   בּוֹאִי בְשָׁלוֹם עֲטֶרֶת בַּעְלָהּ

3. וַהֲבָאַת שָׁלוֹם בֵּין אָדָם לַחֲבֵרוֹ   וַהֲבִיאֵנוּ לְצִיּוֹן עִירְךָ בְּרִנָּה

4. בּוֹאֲכֶם לְשָׁלוֹם מַלְאֲכֵי הַשָּׁלוֹם מַלְאֲכֵי עֶלְיוֹן

5. וּשְׁמֹר צֵאתֵנוּ וּבוֹאֵנוּ לְחַיִּים וּלְשָׁלוֹם מֵעַתָּה וְעַד עוֹלָם

6. וּמַעֲבִיר יוֹם וּמֵבִיא לָיְלָה וּמַבְדִּיל בֵּין יוֹם וּבֵין לָיְלָה

7. וַהֲבִיאֵנוּ לְשָׁלוֹם מֵאַרְבַּע כַּנְפוֹת הָאָרֶץ וְתוֹלִיכֵנוּ קוֹמְמִיּוּת לְאַרְצֵנוּ

Write in the missing letters for these words that are built from the root בוא.

8. בְּ_א   9. וֹ_אֲכֶם   10. וַהֲבִי_ֵנוּ

11. וְהֲ_ָ_את   12. וּמֵבִי_   13. וּב_אֵנוּ

123

The Last Verse of לְכָה דוֹדִי

Your teacher will help you with your translation.

בּוֹאִי בְשָׁלוֹם עֲטֶרֶת בַּעְלָהּ,
גַּם בְּשִׂמְחָה וּבְצָהֳלָה,
תּוֹךְ אֱמוּנֵי עַם סְגֻלָּה,
בֹּאִי כַלָּה, בֹּאִי כַלָּה.

My best guess at the meaning of this prayer is:

_____

_____

_____

_____

Remember

We have learned that there is a tradition that on Shabbat God gives us a **נְשָׁמָה יְתֵרָה**, an extra soul. This is one of the reasons that Shabbat can be a unique experience. This extra soul comes into us when we sing **בֹּאִי כַלָּה**.

Choreography

During the last verse of **לְכָה דוֹדִי** the congregation stands, turns, and faces the door at the words **בֹּאִי כַלָּה, בֹּאִי כַלָּה**. When we do this we are acting as if Shabbat has actually walked in the door and become part of the community.

To Talk About: How does this ritual make a difference? What happens inside us when we stand, turn and bow that would not have happened if we just sat and sang the words?

Side panel

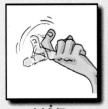
בּוֹא

שָׁלוֹם

שִׂמְחָה

אֱמוּנָה

כַּלָה

Word Parts
in/with = בְּ
and = וְ\וּ

Words
nation = עַם
joy/jubilation = צָהֳלָה
in the middle = תּוֹךְ
treasure = סְגֻלָּה

glory = עֲטֶרֶת
her "husband" = בַּעְלָהּ
also = גַּם

Rebuilding Jerusalem

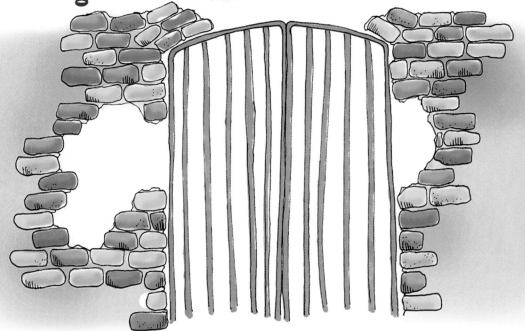

לְכָה דוֹדִי talks about the rebuilding of Jerusalem. Today we have a wonderful modern city of Jerusalem, but that is not the Jerusalem that is being talked about. This Jerusalem is an idea. It is a hope for the future.

The first set of the Ten Commandments was carved by God's own hand on two tablets of stone. When Moses saw the Golden Calf, these tablets fell and broke. Israel did not leave the broken pieces sitting in the desert. They were stored in the Ark of the Covenant along with the second set of tablets that Moses carved with his hand.

Years later, on the same day that the tablets were shattered, the walls of Jerusalem were broken by the Romans.

A teacher named the *Sefat Emet* taught a lesson about the connection between these two breaks. He taught, Both of these breaks need to be healed. These pieces need to be put together again. When the pieces are put back together and these objects made whole, it will be a time of dancing and celebration. Israel will come out of exile. We will be again worthy to have the original Ten Commandments. It will be a time of joy (*Torah Commentary, Balak*).

The idea here is that each of us has to be part of the rebuilding of Jerusalem. Each of us has to help put the pieces back in place. Think about your life. Write three things you hope to contribute to the rebuilding of Jerusalem on these bricks.

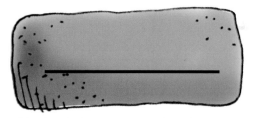
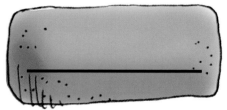
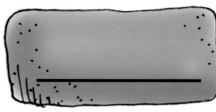

Reviewing לְכָה דוֹדִי

Some things to know about לְכָה דוֹדִי

- לְכָה דוֹדִי is in the center of a service that welcomes Shabbat called קַבָּלַת שַׁבָּת.
- This song speaks of Shabbat as both a Queen and a Bride. We use both of these images to welcome Shabbat.
- לְכָה דוֹדִי speaks of Shabbat, of Jerusalem, and of the Redemption. The idea is that through experiencing Shabbat we get closer to God, gaining resources for rebuilding Jerusalem and bringing the Redemption.

Language Learning

Among the words and word parts we worked with in this unit are:

Roots: בוא זכר שמר

Words:

The Heart of the Prayer

לְכָה דוֹדִי לִקְרַאת כַּלָּה פְּנֵי שַׁבָּת נְקַבְּלָה.

שָׁמוֹר וְזָכוֹר בְּדִבּוּר אֶחָד הִשְׁמִיעָנוּ אֵל הַמְיוּחָד.

יְיָ אֶחָד וּשְׁמוֹ אֶחָד לְשֵׁם וּלְתִפְאֶרֶת וְלִתְהִלָּה.

עֲצֹר!

126

שָׁלוֹם עֲלֵיכֶם

The שַׁבָּת Seder

On Friday night there is a very short service that we do at our dinner table. It can include:

- **Lighting of candles.** Some families light candles at sundown. Some families wait to light candles when they sit down for שַׁבָּת dinner.
  - שָׁלוֹם עֲלֵיכֶם. A song that welcomes angels to our home.
  - **Family blessings.** Parents bless children, and then recite wishes for each other.
  - קִדּוּשׁ. The prayer over wine that makes שַׁבָּת holy.
  - **Washing of hands.**
  - הַמּוֹצִיא. A blessing over bread that begins the meal.

שָׁלוֹם עֲלֵיכֶם

שָׁלוֹם עֲלֵיכֶם is the song we use to welcome שַׁבָּת into our home. It is based on two Talmudic stories that tell us that angels enter our home at the beginning of שַׁבָּת. This song welcomes the angels, invites them in, asks them for a blessing, and then bids them farewell.

שָׁלוֹם עֲלֵיכֶם can be a big family singing opportunity. It is the perfect chance for the kind of loud singing that links people together. It is also the kind of song where people link arms and sway. While we ask angels to bless us with שָׁלוֹם our singing can actually build שַׁבָּת שָׁלוֹם.

In this unit you will learn:
- about שָׁלוֹם עֲלֵיכֶם
- roots בָּרֵךְ ,יָצָא, מָלָה and
- learn the story of the Shabbat angels

שָׁלוֹם עֲלֵיכֶם

PEACE to you	שָׁלוֹם עֲלֵיכֶם	1.
Attending angels	מַלְאֲכֵי הַשָּׁרֵת	2.
Angels who are high up	מַלְאֲכֵי עֶלְיוֹן	3.
From the Ruler, the Ruler of Rulers	מִמֶּלֶךְ מַלְכֵי הַמְּלָכִים	4.
The Holy One.	הַקָּדוֹשׁ בָּרוּךְ הוּא.	5.
COME to us in PEACE	בּוֹאֲכֶם לְשָׁלוֹם	6.
Attending angels	מַלְאֲכֵי הַשָּׁלוֹם	7.
Angels who are high up	מַלְאֲכֵי עֶלְיוֹן	8.
From the Ruler, the Ruler of Rulers	מִמֶּלֶךְ מַלְכֵי הַמְּלָכִים	9.
The Holy One.	הַקָּדוֹשׁ בָּרוּךְ הוּא.	10.
BLESS us with PEACE	בָּרְכוּנִי לְשָׁלוֹם	11.
Attending angels	מַלְאֲכֵי הַשָּׁלוֹם	12.
Angels who are high up	מַלְאֲכֵי עֶלְיוֹן	13.
From the Ruler , the Ruler of Rulers	מִמֶּלֶךְ מַלְכֵי הַמְּלָכִים	14.
The Holy One.	הַקָּדוֹשׁ בָּרוּךְ הוּא.	15.
Take your leave in PEACE	צֵאתְכֶם לְשָׁלוֹם	16.
Attending angels	מַלְאֲכֵי הַשָּׁלוֹם	17.
Angels who are high up	מַלְאֲכֵי עֶלְיוֹן	18.
From the Ruler , the Ruler of Rulers	מִמֶּלֶךְ מַלְכֵי הַמְּלָכִים	19.
The Holy One.	הַקָּדוֹשׁ בָּרוּךְ הוּא.	20.

Root Review

Review these root words and practice the phrases below.

Can you see the three letters מלך in these words?

ruler = מֶלֶךְ

the rulers = הַמְּלָכִים

1. יי מֶלֶךְ יי מָלָךְ יי יִמְלֹךְ   בָּרוּךְ שֵׁם כְּבוֹד מַלְכוּתוֹ לְעוֹלָם וָעֶד

2. יַחַד כֻּלָּם הוֹדוּ וְהִמְלִיכוּ וְאָמְרוּ   מֶלֶךְ מַלְכֵי הַמְּלָכִים הַקָּדוֹשׁ בָּרוּךְ הוּא

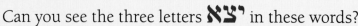

Can you see the three letters יצא in these words?

going out = יְצִיאָה

leave = צֵאתְכֶם

3. הַמּוֹצִיא לֶחֶם מִן הָאָרֶץ   בְּצֵאת יִשְׂרָאֵל מִמִּצְרָיִם בֵּית יַעֲקֹב

4. צֵאתְכֶם לְשָׁלוֹם מַלְאֲכֵי הַשָּׁלוֹם   אֲשֶׁר הוֹצֵאתִי אֶתְכֶם מֵאֶרֶץ מִצְרָיִם

Can you see the three letters ברך in these words?

blessed = בָּרוּךְ

bless me = בָּרְכוּנִי

5. בָּרוּךְ יי הַמְבֹרָךְ לְעוֹלָם וָעֶד   בָּרְכוּנִי לְשָׁלוֹם מַלְאֲכֵי הַשָּׁלוֹם מַלְאֲכֵי עֶלְיוֹן

6. וַאֲבָרְכָה שִׁמְךָ לְעוֹלָם וָעֶד   וַאֲנַחְנוּ נְבָרֵךְ יָהּ מֵעַתָּה וְעַד עוֹלָם הַלְלוּיָהּ

שָׁלוֹם

עַל

מַלְאָךְ

מֶלֶךְ

קָדוֹשׁ

בָּרוּךְ

Your teacher will help you with your translation.

שָׁלוֹם עֲלֵיכֶם מַלְאֲכֵי הַשָּׁרֵת מַלְאֲכֵי עֶלְיוֹן מִמֶּלֶךְ מַלְכֵי הַמְּלָכִים הַקָּדוֹשׁ בָּרוּךְ הוּא

My best guess at the meaning of this prayer is:

_____

_____

_____

Word Parts		Words
you (plural) = כֶם■	of (plural) = י ■	service = שָׁרֵת
the = הַ	from = מִ	high = עֶלְיוֹן
		He = הוּא

130

The Shabbat Angels

Two angels visit Jewish homes every Friday night. When they arrive at the house they check to see if the Shabbat candles are lit, if the table is set, and if there is a sense of שְׁלוֹם־בַּיִת (family peace). They want to know if Shabbat has been "made" in this home.

If there is a feeling of Shabbat in the house, the good angel says, "May this family have a Shabbat like this every week!" and the evil angel is forced to say "Amen."

But if there is no feeling of Shabbat in the house, the evil angel says, "May this family have a Shabbat like this every week!" and the good angel is forced to say "Amen" (*Shabbat* 119b).

Questions
1. What lesson can we learn from the "good angel's" blessing?
2. What lesson can we learn from the "evil angel's" blessing?
3. How can knowing this story help us to point our hearts when we sing שָׁלוֹם עֲלֵיכֶם?

131

Reading Your Way Through שַׁבָּת

Here are some phrases to practice from prayers we say on שַׁבָּת.

1. לְכָה דוֹדִי לִקְרַאת כַּלָה   פְּנֵי שַׁבָּת נְקַבְּלָה

2. עַל יַד אִישׁ בֶּן־פַּרְצִי וְנִשְׂמְחָה וְנָגִילָה   בֹּאִי כַלָה בֹּאִי כַלָה

3. בֵּינִי וּבֵין בְּנֵי־יִשְׂרָאֵל אוֹת הִיא לְעֹלָם   כִּי שֵׁשֶׁת־יָמִים עָשָׂה יי

4. בָּרְכוּנִי לְשָׁלוֹם מַלְאֲכֵי הַשָּׁלוֹם   שָׁמוֹר וְזָכוֹר בְּדִבּוּר אֶחָד

5. מִזְמוֹר שִׁיר לְיוֹם הַשַּׁבָּת   מֶלֶךְ מַלְכֵי הַמְּלָכִים

6. צֵאתְכֶם לְשָׁלוֹם מַלְאֲכֵי הַשָּׁלוֹם   הַקָּדוֹשׁ בָּרוּךְ הוּא

7. וְשָׁמְרוּ בְנֵי־יִשְׂרָאֵל אֶת־הַשַּׁבָּת   יָמִין וּשְׂמֹאל תִּפְרֹצִי

8. עָשָׂה יי אֶת־הַשָּׁמַיִם וְאֶת־הָאָרֶץ וּבַיּוֹם הַשְּׁבִיעִי שָׁבַת וַיִּנָּפַשׁ

9. בֹּאִי בְשָׁלוֹם עֲטֶרֶת בַּעְלָהּ גַּם בְּשִׂמְחָה וּבְצָהֳלָה

10. שָׁלוֹם עֲלֵיכֶם מַלְאֲכֵי הַשָּׁרֵת מַלְאֲכֵי עֶלְיוֹן מִמֶּלֶךְ מַלְכֵי הַמְּלָכִים

11. מִקְדַּשׁ מֶלֶךְ עִיר מְלוּכָה, קוּמִי צְאִי מִתּוֹךְ הַהֲפֵכָה

12. לִקְרַאת שַׁבָּת לְכוּ וְנֵלְכָה, כִּי הִיא מְקוֹר הַבְּרָכָה

13. בּוֹאֲכֶם לְשָׁלוֹם מַלְאֲכֵי הַשָּׁלוֹם מַלְאֲכֵי עֶלְיוֹן מִמֶּלֶךְ מַלְכֵי הַמְּלָכִים

The כֶם Ending

כֶם means you (plural). Match the word in the right column with its mate with the כֶם ending.

צֵאתְכֶם	נֶפֶשׁ
עֵינֵיכֶם	בּוֹא
בּוֹאֲכֶם	יָצָא
נַפְשְׁכֶם	עֵינַיִם

The next three verses of שָׁלוֹם עֲלֵיכֶם are the same except for the first word.

בּוֹאֲכֶם לְשָׁלוֹם מַלְאֲכֵי הַשָּׁלוֹם מַלְאֲכֵי עֶלְיוֹן

בָּרְכוּנִי לְשָׁלוֹם מַלְאֲכֵי הַשָּׁלוֹם מַלְאֲכֵי עֶלְיוֹן

צֵאתְכֶם לְשָׁלוֹם מַלְאֲכֵי הַשָּׁלוֹם מַלְאֲכֵי עֶלְיוֹן

Your teacher will help you with your translation.

בּוֹא

שָׁלוֹם

מַלְאָךְ

My best guess at the meaning of this prayer is:

_____

_____

_____

יָצָא

בָּרוּךְ

Words

on high = עֶלְיוֹן

Word Parts

you (plural) = כֶם■

me = נִי■

133

The Other שַׁבָּת Angels Story

In the Talmud is a second, very short story about the שַׁבָּת angels.

If a person prays on עֶרֶב שַׁבָּת (Friday night), two angels walk with him, place their hands on his head, and say, "God will forgive you for whatever you have done wrong" (*Shabbat* 119b).

Questions

1. Why does celebrating שַׁבָּת help God to forgive us?

2. How can knowing this story help us to point our hearts when we sing שָׁלוֹם עֲלֵיכֶם?

Reviwing שָׁלוֹם עֲלֵיכֶם

Some things to know about שָׁלוֹם עֲלֵיכֶם

This prayer is based on the Talmudic story of angels that come to visit Jewish homes on Friday night.

It is part of the שַׁבָּת seder, the Friday night table service.

Language Learning

Among the words and word parts we worked with in this unit are:

Roots:

Words:

שָׁלוֹם	עַל	מַלְאָךְ	מֶלֶךְ	קָדוֹשׁ	בָּרוּךְ	בּוֹא

The Heart of the Prayer

שָׁלוֹם עֲלֵיכֶם מַלְאֲכֵי הַשָּׁרֵת מַלְאֲכֵי עֶלְיוֹן

מִמֶּלֶךְ מַלְכֵי הַמְּלָכִים הַקָּדוֹשׁ בָּרוּךְ הוּא

עֲצֹר!

Unit 12 בִּרְכַת הַמָּזוֹן

בִּרְכַת הַמָּזוֹן means "the blessing of the food." It is said after eating. It is sometimes called "The Grace after Eating."

Some things to know about בִּרְכַת הַמָּזוֹן are:

It should be said at the table where you ate.

When three or more people say it together, it begins with an invitation and response that is very much like the בָּרְכוּ.

There are actually four blessings in בִּרְכַת הַמָּזוֹן and extra pieces that one does on Shabbat and holidays (but we are only going to look at the first paragraph).

Each of the בְּרָכוֹת tells a story, and when you put them together they retell the history of the Jewish people.

Here are the four stories:

1. Moses wrote the בְּרָכָה: "*The One-Who-Feeds all*" when God first fed Israel with manna.

2. Joshua wrote the בְּרָכָה: "*For the land and for the food*" when the people of Israel first entered the Promised Land.

3. David and Solomon wrote the בְּרָכָה: "*The One-Who-in-kindness-Rebuilds Jerusalem.*" David wrote, "On Israel Your people and on Jerusalem Your city." Solomon wrote, "And on Your great and holy house".

4. The last בְּרָכָה, "*The One-Who-is-good and does good,*" was written after a small miracle made things slightly better after the defeat of Bar Kokhba. A moment of major Jewish sadness showed one good thing (*Brakhot* 48a).

When we say בִּרְכַת הַמָּזוֹן we turn every table into a place of worship.

Question: Why is a table a great place to pray?

In this unit you will learn:
- about בִּרְכַת הַמָּזוֹן
- the roots ז ו ן, רחם, חסד
- three stories

135

בִּרְכַּת הַמָּזוֹן

Blessed be You ADONAI	בָּרוּךְ אַתָּה יי	1.
Our God, Ruler of the Cosmos	אֱלֹהֵינוּ מֶלֶךְ הָעוֹלָם	2.
The ONE-Who-sustains the whole cosmos with GOODNESS	הַזָּן אֶת־הָעוֹלָם כֻּלּוֹ בְּטוּבוֹ	3.
With GRACIOUSNESS and KINDNESS and COMPASSION.	בְּחֵן בְּחֶסֶד וּבְרַחֲמִים.	4.
God gives BREAD to all creatures.	הוּא נוֹתֵן לֶחֶם לְכָל־בָּשָׂר	5.
God's KINDNESS endures forever.	כִּי לְעוֹלָם חַסְדּוֹ.	6.
Your great GOODNESS	וּבְטוּבוֹ הַגָּדוֹל	7.
has never failed us	תָּמִיד לֹא חָסַר לָנוּ	8.
Don't take FOOD away from us	וְאַל יֶחְסַר לָנוּ מָזוֹן	9.
forever and always.	לְעוֹלָם וָעֶד	10.
For the sake of your great NAME	בַּעֲבוּר שְׁמוֹ הַגָּדוֹל	11.
Because you are the God of NOURISHMENT	כִּי הוּא אֵל זָן	12.
and You SUSTAIN all	וּמְפַרְנֵס לַכֹּל	13.
and You are GOOD to all	וּמֵטִיב לַכֹּל	14.
and you provide NOURISHMENT	וּמֵכִין מָזוֹן	15.
to all your creatures that You CREATED.	לְכָל־בְּרִיּוֹתָיו אֲשֶׁר בָּרָא.	16.
Praised are You ADONAI	בָּרוּךְ אַתָּה יי	17.
The ONE-Who-NOURISHES all.	הַזָּן אֶת־הַכֹּל.	18.

Do your remember this three-letter root חסד?

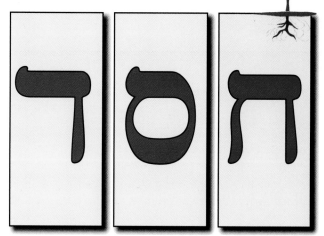

חֶסֶד   חַסְדֵי   חֲסָדִים

kindness = חֶסֶד

kindness of = חַסְדֵי

acts of = גְּמִילוּת חֲסָדִים
loving kindness

Practice these words and circle all the words that contain the root חסד.

1. וְזוֹכֵר חַסְדֵי אָבוֹת וְאִמָּהוֹת   כֻּלּוֹ בְּטוּבוֹ בְּחֵן בְּחֶסֶד וּבְרַחֲמִים

2. וְהַמְרַחֵם כִּי לֹא תַמּוּ חֲסָדֶיךָ   אֱלֹהִים בְּרֹב חַסְדֶּךָ עֲנֵנִי בֶּאֱמֶת יִשְׁעֶךָ

Can you see the three letters רחם in these words?

רֶחֶם   רַחֵם   הָרַחֲמָן

womb = רֶחֶם

mercy = רַחֵם

the Merciful One = הָרַחֲמָן

Practice these phrases and circle all the words that contain the root רחם.

3. אַב הָרַחֲמִים הֵיטִיבָה בִרְצוֹנְךָ   יְיָ יְיָ אֵל רַחוּם וְחַנּוּן אֶרֶךְ אַפַּיִם

4. כִּי אֵל מֶלֶךְ חַנּוּן וְרַחוּם אָתָּה   רַחֵם עַל צִיּוֹן כִּי הִיא בֵּית חַיֵּינוּ

5. הָאָב הָרַחֲמָן הַמְרַחֵם רַחֵם עָלֵינוּ   וְרַחֲמָיו עַל כָּל־מַעֲשָׂיו

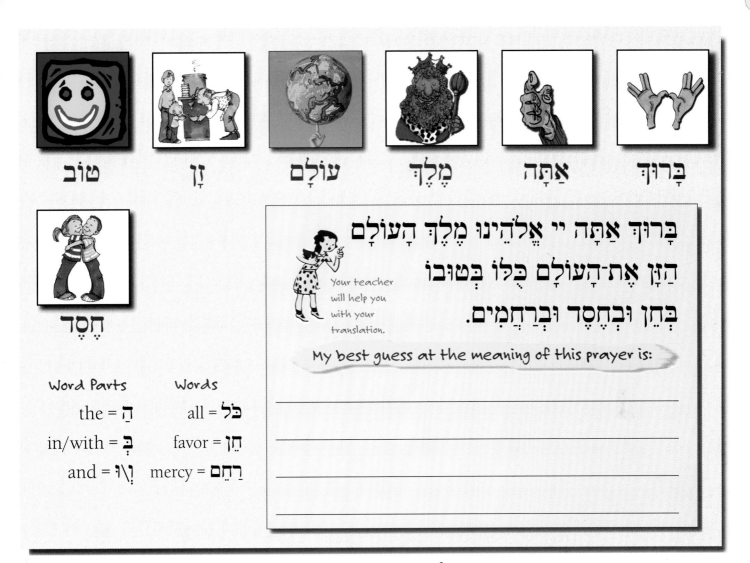

טוֹב   זָן   עוֹלָם   מֶלֶךְ   אַתָּה   בָּרוּךְ

חֶסֶד

בָּרוּךְ אַתָּה יי אֱלֹהֵינוּ מֶלֶךְ הָעוֹלָם

הַזָּן אֶת־הָעוֹלָם כֻּלּוֹ בְּטוּבוֹ

בְּחֵן וּבְחֶסֶד וּבְרַחֲמִים.

Your teacher will help you with your translation.

My best guess at the meaning of this prayer is:

_____

_____

_____

_____

Word Parts

the = הַ

in/with = בְּ

and = וְ\וּ

Words

all = כֹּל

favor = חֵן

mercy = רַחֵם

Practicing More of בִּרְכַּת הַמָּזוֹן

Now practice the next two parts of בִּרְכַּת הַמָּזוֹן.

1. נוֹדֶה לְךָ, יי אֱלֹהֵינוּ, עַל שֶׁהִנְחַלְתָּ לַאֲבוֹתֵינוּ אֶרֶץ חֶמְדָּה טוֹבָה וּרְחָבָה,

2. וְעַל שֶׁהוֹצֵאתָנוּ, יי אֱלֹהֵינוּ, מֵאֶרֶץ מִצְרַיִם, וּפְדִיתָנוּ מִבֵּית עֲבָדִים,

3. וְעַל בְּרִיתְךָ שֶׁחָתַמְתָּ בִּבְשָׂרֵנוּ, וְעַל תּוֹרָתְךָ שֶׁלִּמַּדְתָּנוּ, וְעַל חֻקֶּיךָ שֶׁהוֹדַעְתָּנוּ,

4. וְעַל חַיִּים חֵן וָחֶסֶד שֶׁחוֹנַנְתָּנוּ, וְעַל אֲכִילַת מָזוֹן שָׁאַתָּה זָן וּמְפַרְנֵס אוֹתָנוּ תָּמִיד,

5. בְּכָל־יוֹם וּבְכָל־עֵת וּבְכָל־שָׁעָה.

6. וְעַל הַכֹּל, יי אֱלֹהֵינוּ, אֲנַחְנוּ מוֹדִים לָךְ, וּמְבָרְכִים אוֹתָךְ, יִתְבָּרַךְ שִׁמְךָ

7. בְּפִי כָל־חַי תָּמִיד לְעוֹלָם וָעֶד, כַּכָּתוּב: וְאָכַלְתָּ וְשָׂבָעְתָּ וּבֵרַכְתָּ אֶת־יי אֱלֹהֶיךָ

8. עַל הָאָרֶץ הַטּוֹבָה אֲשֶׁר נָתַן לָךְ. בָּרוּךְ אַתָּה יי, עַל הָאָרֶץ וְעַל הַמָּזוֹן.

About Manna

Israel spent forty years in the desert. God made manna rain down six days a week. Manna was the special food which fed them in the desert. God made twice as much manna fall on Fridays. God let no manna fall on Shabbat. The two _hallot_ on the Friday night table remind us of the double portion of manna that was stockpiled for Shabbat.

Rabbi Shimon Bar Yoḥai's students asked, Why did God make manna fall daily rather than falling only once a year and providing a year's worth?

Rabbi Shimon Bar Yoḥai told this story: Once there was a king who gave his son an allowance big enough to last a whole year. Therefore, the prince came to visit his father only once a year to pick up his money. The king got lonely so he changed the plan. He switched the annual allowance to a daily allowance and got to see his son every day (_Yoma_ 76a).

Questions

1. Why was the falling of manna the moment when the first blessing בִּרְכַּת הַמָּזוֹן was said?
2. Rabbi Shimon bar Yoḥai taught that each day the manna fell was a new chance to get close to God. How is the same true of every meal we eat?
3. The Families-of-Israel knew that the manna came directly from God. How can we know that God is involved in the meals we eat?
4. How can knowing about manna help us to know where to point our hearts when we say בִּרְכַּת הַמָּזוֹן?

עֲצֹר!

Can you see the three letters זון in these words?

מֵזִין   מָזוֹן   זָן

Hebrew builds words out of three-letter roots.

feeds = זָן

food = מָזוֹן

provide sustenance = מֵזִין

Practice these phrases and circle all the words that contain the root זון.

1. בָּרוּךְ אַתָּה יי הַזָּן אֶת־הַכֹּל   וּמֵטִיב לַכֹּל וּמֵכִין מָזוֹן

2. חֹמֶר מֵזִין וְטוֹב לַבְּרִיאוּת   בּוֹרֵא מִינֵי מְזוֹנוֹת

A Visit to Heaven and Hell

A very righteous man died. The angels offered him a choice between heaven and hell. He said, I've never been there, how can I choose? The angels offered him a visit to each. First, he was taken to a banquet hall loaded with food. It was the ultimate feast. Out came sad, very skinny people who walked to the tables filled with food and just stood there. They could not eat because on one hand was tied a giant fork and on the other a giant spoon. This was hell.

Then he was taken to a second hall, also loaded with food. Out came happy people; well-fed people who were singing and dancing. They walked to the tables. On their hands were tied the same huge spoons and forks. When they reached the tables they picked up the food in their giant silverware and lifted it to their neighbors' mouths. When the man was offered his choice again, he chose hell. He said, Now I know the secret of how to turn it into heaven *(a Jewish folktale)*.

Questions
1. What lessons can you learn from this story?
2. The Torah tells us that "God feeds everyone. How can we be like God?
3. The first blessing in בִּרְכַּת הַמָּזוֹן ends with the idea that "God feeds everyone. How can knowing this story help you point your heart when you say בִּרְכַּת הַמָּזוֹן?

140

Your teacher will help you with your translation.

כִּי הוּא אֵל זָן וּמְפַרְנֵס לַכֹּל
וּמֵטִיב לַכֹּל וּמֵכִין מָזוֹן
לְכָל־בְּרִיּוֹתָיו אֲשֶׁר בָּרָא.
בָּרוּךְ אַתָּה יי הַזָּן אֶת־הַכֹּל.

My best guess at the meaning of this prayer is:

_____

_____

_____

_____

זָן

טוֹב

בָּרוּךְ

אַתָּה

Words

because = כִּי
He (God) = הוּא
provides = מְפַרְנֵס
all/everything = כֹּל
prepare = מֵכִין
creatures = בְּרִיּוֹת
that = אֲשֶׁר
created = בָּרָא

Word Parts

the = הַ
to = לְ
and = וְ\וּ
His (plural) = יו ▪

Abraham's Two Mitzvot

The Midrash tells two different stories that connect Abraham to בִּרְכַּת הַמָּזוֹן.

[1] Abraham had a tent with four doors, one pointing in each direction. That way, no one looking for hospitality would ever have to look for a way in. He would feed them and offer them a place to stay.

[2] After dinner, Abraham would invite his guests to join him in thanking God for the food and shelter that God had provided. Abraham tried to teach them that even though he was sharing food with them, it really came from God. In this way, Abraham was the first person to say בִּרְכַּת הַמָּזוֹן (*Gen. R.* 48.9; 49.7; 39.21).

Questions

1. How can בִּרְכַּת הַמָּזוֹן help us to remember to feed people who are hungry?

2. How can בִּרְכַּת הַמָּזוֹן help us teach other people about God?

3. How can this story help you to point your heart when you say בִּרְכַּת הַמָּזוֹן?

The Twelve Loaves

In 1492 many Jews had to leave Spain because of the Spanish Inquisition. Two of them were Esperanza and her husband, the tailor, Jacobo. When they left their home in Spain they decided to go home. They went to the Land of Israel and settled in the city of Tzfat, the place that was becoming the new center for Kabbalah. Jacobo set up a tailor shop. On his first Shabbat he went to the synagogue on Shabbat morning. This Shabbat was the rabbi's sixtieth birthday. He gave a sermon about the twelve loaves of Shew Bread that the tribes put in the Temple before each Shabbat. Jacobo did not understand much of the sermon, but he did understand clearly that the rabbi said that   God liked the smell of the bread.

When he told Esperanza about the sermon she came up with an idea. She said,   I will bake twelve loaves of *pan de Dios* (the bread of God), and we will offer them as a gift of thanksgiving.   When Shabbat was over, she began to bake. In the middle of the night Jacobo brought the loaves to the synagogue and left them in the ark. He said a prayer thanking God for the good things that had happened to them. Then he went home.

A little while later the *shammas*, the man who worked for the synagogue, came in to start to get things ready for the service. He cried to God while he worked. He said, I have not been paid in many weeks.

He yelled at God, I am doing Your work, taking care of Your house and my family is hungry. You need to do something. When he started to clean the ark he found the *hallot* and thanked God for the help.

Thirty years went by. Every week Esperanza baked *hallah*. Every week Jacobo brought it to the synagogue and thanked God. Every week God gave the *shammas* and his family food. On the rabbi's ninetieth birthday he decided to give another sermon on the Shew Bread. He stayed late on Saturday night, using the library at the back of the sanctuary to do research. When Jacobo came in, he listened to his prayer and then yelled at him, Fool, people do not feed God. When the two of them heard the *shammas* coming, they hid. When the *shammas* took the *hallot* out of the ark, the rabbi called him a thief, saying, That food belongs to God.

The three men were yelling at each other when the door opened. In walked the Holy Ari, the great Kabbalist, who said, God sent me here to tell you the following. People can really share what they have with God, and with their help, God really is הַזָּן אֶת-הַכּל, the One-Who-feeds all (*From a story by Shlomo Carelbach as first heard from Art Green and then retold by the author over thirty years*).

Questions
1. How can people share what they have with God?
2. How can God feed people?
3. How can knowing this story help you know where to point your heart when you say the בִּרְכַּת הַמָּזוֹן?

143

Reviewing בִּרְכַּת הַמָּזוֹן

Some things to know about בִּרְכַּת הַמָּזוֹן:

- It is a way of turning a table into a place of worship.
- When three or more people say it, it changes and becomes a way of building community.
- It is an imitation of what Abraham used to do with strangers.
- It tells four stories: (a) manna falling in the wilderness, (b) entering the land of Israel, (c) taking Jerusalem and building the Temple, and (d) starting over after the Bar Kokhba revolt against Rome fails.

Language Learning:

Among the words and word parts we worked with in this unit are:

Roots: זון חסד רחם

Words:

זָן   חֶסֶד   טוֹב   עוֹלָם   מֶלֶךְ   אַתָּה   בָּרוּךְ

The Heart of the Prayer: בָּרוּךְ אַתָּה יי הַזָּן אֶת-הַכֹּל